Letters
from
Amelia

LETTERS FROM AMELIA

1901–1937

Jean L. Backus

Beacon Press   Boston

Photographs courtesy Schlesinger Library, Radcliffe College, Jean L. Backus, and Mrs. Muriel Earhart Morrissey

Beacon Press books are published under the auspices of the Unitarian Universalist Association, 25 Beacon Street, Boston, Massachusetts 02108 Published simultaneously in Canada by Fitzhenry & Whiteside Limited, Toronto

Printed in the United States of America

(hardcover) 9 8 7 6 5 4 3 2 1

Library of Congress Cataloging in Publication Data

Earhart, Amelia, 1897-1937.
 Letters from Amelia, 1901–1937.

 1. Earhart, Amelia, 1897-1937. 2. Women air pilots — United States — Correspondence.
I. Backus, Jean L. II. Title.
TL540.E3A4 1982 629.13'092'4 [B] 81-68356
ISBN 0-8070-6702-4 AACR2

To Lois and Helen

"It is so good to think she was known and loved over so much of the world and deserved it, for she was straight and simple..."

Amy Otis Earhart, letter
to a friend, August 1937

"I have great affection for Amelia, she is a grand person and should never be forgotten."

Eleanor Roosevelt, letter
to Amy Otis Earhart, March 1938

Contents

Letters
from
Amelia

ONE

Golden Girl
1982

Amelia Earhart, the world's most famous woman pilot, would be eighty-five years old now. She would exult over social freedoms and programs undreamed of in her time. She would be fascinated by outer space and anxious to fly there — if she hadn't already visited the moon. She would be as visionary and as practical, as innovative and as conservative, as courageous and as modest as she was in the days before her disappearance in 1937.

Her 1928 flight as a passenger from America to England made her the first woman ever to fly the North Atlantic, her 1932 flight made her the first woman ever to fly it twice and to fly it solo. These are the most impressive of many records she broke and rebroke during her career, which only lasted for nine years. In life she captured the attention of the world with her exploits as well as her distinctive qualities, and in death she seems destined to hold it forever.

Amelia Earhart's appearance was too singular to represent conventional feminine beauty, but it pleased and satisfied admirers and so impressed her publisher that in time he not only made her his wife but publicized her so well she became a standard of beauty on her own account. The leggy strength of her slim body, the direct glance from clear blue eyes, as full of wonder as a child's, the cropped hair, the cheerful grin, the breezy manner — the clichés multiplied and were widely imitated by girls and women who adopted the "Amelia Look."

She was a solitary, happiest alone in the air or in a greasy monkeysuit at work with the men on her beloved Lockheed. Yet she designed appealing clothes for women and wore them with style, whether meeting British royalty or enjoying a family meal with the President of the United States at the White House. Her energy was abundant, and after the 1928 flight she gathered crowds everywhere she went, adoring fans who came to gaze, to listen, if possible to touch, and always to echo her message across the land: Flying is safe, and women make good pilots.

Her career certainly, and probably her life, came to an end on July 2, 1937, somewhere in the vicinity of remote Howland Island, almost 2600 miles from Lae, New Guinea, 7000 miles short of making her the first woman to fly around the world, and twenty-two days before her fortieth birthday. In whatever form she met death, she undoubtedly faced it as courageously as she had faced other painful, difficult, or dangerous situations. Since there were no more oceans to cross, no more uncharted areas to explore, nothing more venturesome to attempt than following paths developed by expanding airlines, from her point of view if she "popped off" on this ultimate flight it would still be worthwhile and would present the best death she could wish for. She said so more than once.

Certainly the circumstances of her disappearance added drama and preserved her fame at its peak. "Whatever happened to Amelia Earhart?" became a mystery which has fascinated searchers, writers, sensationalists, theorists, militarists, romanticists, and many others ever since. No one knows now, and it is unlikely anyone will ever discover the truth of that day in the vastness of the Pacific Ocean.

With time, the reality of Amelia Earhart has given way to the romanticized image, larger than life, which is now fixed in the public mind. Was she really only a golden girl with a good adviser and manager? Or an unapproachable intellectual and prickly female, as she was considered by some, who adopted male attire and habits to show the world women could fly any plane anywhere as well as any man could? "A concoction of media hype and good luck," Pete Hamill called her in a 1976 article for *Ms.*, but he concluded, "she was a genuine hero in the end."

To gain a perspective on the reality of this heroine is to examine the uncommon means by which she satisfied needs and desires common to most people. At a time when women were restricted to domesticity, she fled from it. When they were considered only fit for motherhood, she refused it. When fidelity was a convention of marriage, she denied it. When business was dominated by men, she competed. When records were established, she broke them. And when men flew, she flew too, satisfying an atavistic desire to free herself from earth's tether, to reach the sun, to spin out toward eternity even if she were never to come back.

Her ego was strong enough to balance her differences from other people against her similarities, and her moderate opinion of her accomplishments and worth denied any exceptional qualities. If she could do it, any woman could. Her will was almost as strong as her ego, and equally reasonable. She controlled it by honestly viewing and reviewing what she had and what she wanted, what she could get and what she would have to do without. She weighed cause against effect, studied all angles of a problem before coming to a decision, and prepared her flights meticulously. She formed judgments and drew conclusions without recourse to emotion. Yet she was warmly affectionate with her family and friends, and only rarely admitted that the responsibility she voluntarily assumed for some of them was a burden. In her opinion, to do this was only a matter of conscience and loyalty to one's kin or comrades, however improvident and undeserving they might be.

Not everyone loved Amelia Earhart. She was said by some friends and all her foes at one time or another to be withdrawn, cold, greedy, self-serving, patronizing, arrogant, and supercilious, among other epithets. Jealousy and resentment motivated some women and some men pilots against her; some of the family thought her too nonconformist to be acceptable, though all of them doted on gossip about her and a good many became her financial dependents. She disliked intimacy so intensely she closed up when would-be intimates came too near, and she was so impatient of sentimentality she often disdained genuine though superficial emotions in others. Although her attitude is better defined as affectionate annoyance, she appeared to patronize her mother and sister, probably from a misperception that they had distanced themselves from her, when in reality it was she who had left their vicinity. Her schedules were so tight, she sometimes appeared rude and ungracious to those who were courteous to her or who pre- ·sumed on old acquaintance or collateral family relations. On the other hand, she was forever relating herself to the past, telling how some old friend or distant cousin had turned up to greet her in public.

She had the good fortune to be of the correct age, sex, and breeding, and to possess not only the dedication to aviation but the official credentials for flying, when a highly presentable American woman pilot was required for the 1928 flight to England. After the fame and glory, which brought no financial reward, she realized that only money would secure what she'd need to fulfill her professional dreams, and she married the man who could abundantly help her secure it. She spoke of her marriage as a partnership, and never denied that her husband's ability to acquire funding for her flying was one reason she had chosen him.

For George Palmer Putnam of the old and respected publishing firm, she really was the golden girl. He sold her to the world when he published her first book, *20 Hrs. 40 Min.*, scooping other publishers as he had the year before when he brought out *We* by Colonel Charles A. Lindbergh. A year later the publisher divorced his wife, the mother of his two sons, and married his client.

Amelia's sister, Muriel Earhart Morrissey, when any question of sibling rivalry was mentioned to her, strongly denied it. Deeply devoted to her own family and involved with church and a teaching career, Muriel wrote *Courage Is the Price*, her story of two little girls born of loving parents. One grew up to be a world-famous pilot and the other stayed home to raise a family. If occasionally the connection between the sisters grew strained, the remarkable woman who was their mother stepped in to ease the tension, and on occasion unwittingly to exacerbate it.

Amy Otis Earhart was born with a generous spirit and great physical stamina, although her hearing was impaired from the age of sixteen. Raised in a social milieu which held fast to its standards and conventions, she never remarried after her divorce in 1924 from Edwin Stanton Earhart, yet she was daring enough and loving enough to support Amelia's desire to fly. She gave part of the money for Amelia's first plane, and later was a fearless passenger with her daughter at the controls. Frequently Amelia related during a lecture how her mother would read a book when they were flying together.

Amy was staying at the Putnam's North Hollywood residence when Amelia vanished in 1937, and she remained there for some time afterward, with frequent but short visits to Muriel and other relatives in the East and Midwest. A number of times she moved temporarily to Berkeley, California, and in July 1949, she became a paying guest in an old brown-shingled house growing out of a canyon hillside behind the town. Every evening at sunset she went to stand on a balcony, gazing west past the University of California and the bay of San Francisco toward the Pacific, where she expected Amelia to appear from her round-the-world flight. No recall of the twelve years since her daughter's disappearance could persuade Mrs. Earhart that the flight had probably ended when the Lockheed Electra slid with empty gas tanks beneath the waves. No recounting of the various official and private searches, no repetition of theories about espionage, capture, and execution, nor any reprise of World War II, could change her belief that the plane would eventually fly in over the Golden Gate.

But it never did, and no one knows when Mrs. Earhart accepted the fact that Amelia would never return. After a year in Berkeley she moved East to live permanently with Muriel in Medford, Massachusetts, where she died on October 29, 1962, in her nineties.

No one realized that left behind were four cardboard cartons of letters and miscellanea, which remained undisturbed and unclaimed until the owner of the brown-shingled house died in 1975. Her heir then called a secondhand book dealer to evaluate the large library, and other items in the attic. When he saw the cartons and learned they contained material relating to Amelia Earhart, he offered a large sum to buy them unopened.

As a friend of both the owner and the heir, I was then asked to examine the contents before the cartons were sold. The first thing I discovered was that Mrs. Earhart had saved literally everything, from her own wedding invitation to notes found in floating bottles after Amelia's disappearance. She saved telegrams, get-well and Christmas cards, Easter greetings and gift tags, wedding and birth announcements, and newspaper clippings, many of them. A torn and empty package wrapping had contained "AE's mudstained and moth-eaten jodhpurs," and another equally empty package was marked "Destroy without opening." Crayon drawings from her Morrissey grandchildren were side by side with photographs which Amy believed had been taken "of AE by AE when she was studying commercial photography."

Jumbled in every which way were more than a hundred long letters and short notes from Amelia to her mother. Filled with family gossip, itineraries, financial discussions, comments on religion, birth control, and marriage, the letters begin with a note from Amelia at four years of age to her Grandmother Otis. They end with what may have been the last written word to her mother in 1937. Since she rarely dated her letters except by day of the week, and since some postmarks were torn off or smudged, cataloguing the collection and segregating other letters and material in the four cartons was difficult and took more than eight months.

Sometimes the letter contents were the only clue to date or relevance, or were no clue at all, and some of the envelopes were empty. In some instances I used a perpetual calendar to determine as accurately as possible where a letter belonged in the chronology, and all dates I supplied I have enclosed in brackets. Although several letters were unsigned, it was no problem to identify Amelia's difficult handwriting, only to decipher her meaning.

When complete, the collection presented the human side of a great woman with all her virtues and imperfections, a woman of enormous public acclaim and heroic accomplishment, and a woman who never failed in her obligations as a devoted daughter, a supportive sister, and a liberated wife.

I found no new information concerning the disappearance, but the letters, besides being a pleasure to read, expanded my interest and curiosity in the immediate ancestors and societal milieu of which she was the product, as well as the great sources of strength which enabled her to leave her imprint on aviation and on women everywhere.

TWO

Atchison, Kansas 1901-1908

On July 24, 1901, her fourth birthday, Millie printed her first letter.

> DEAR GRANDMA. I GOT A STOVE WITH A TEA KETTLE AND
> PAN. A DOLL AND SOME BOOKS. I LOVE YOU AND THANK
> YOU. YOUR LOVING MILLIE.

"Millie" was Amelia Mary Earhart, who one day would be the most famous woman pilot in the world, and who in 1937 would vanish into a central Pacific mist of conjecture which has never been dispelled.

"Grandma" was Amelia Harres Otis, wife of Judge Alfred Otis of Atchison, Kansas, for whom Millie was named. These maternal grandparents provided for Amelia and her younger sister Muriel Grace a socially conservative background founded on ancestor worship and material gain. Grandpa Otis was overly proud of his New England heritage, which included that James Otis who proposed the Stamp Act Congress in 1765, an event said to have begun the American Revolution. The Judge was now retired from the bench but still president of the Atchison Savings Bank, and immensely wealthy from shrewd land speculation.

In 1854, when passage of the Kansas-Nebraska Act divided what had been a raw and wild part of the Louisiana Purchase, antislavery proponents formed the Emigrant Aid Company for the purpose of organizing immigration into the new Territory of Kansas. Among the settlers was Alfred Gideon Otis, a young lawyer born in the state of New York and educated in Michigan. He and several young friends, including a future state governor and a United States senator, chose to settle in Atchison, which had been a stopping place for westbound Conestoga caravans during the Gold Rush to California. They staked claims to the best land, and in the course of building a town frequently aided runaway slaves from Missouri. All later served the Union in the Civil War.

Kansas was admitted as a Free State in 1861, and the following year, Alfred Otis went East to marry Amelia Josephine Harres of Philadelphia, a Quaker whom he brought West by train to St. Louis and then down the Missouri River by steamer. "Not in a covered wagon," as their daughter Amy would one day remark indignantly. Even so, Indians still roamed Atchison freely, and Main Street was not yet paved.

On a bluff called Quality Hill overlooking the great bend of the river, Judge Otis built a handsome nine-room house of brick and frame for his bride, and every time one of their eight children was born, a new room was added. Amy would remember crystal chandeliers and a piano in the drawing room, many well-read books in the library, and four-posters in the bedrooms upstairs. There were Irish maids and cooks, and men to keep the riding and carriage horses in the large barn and to tend the extensive gardens.

By 1900 Atchison was an important rail center, dating from 1872 when Atchison, Topeka and Santa Fe completed laying track to this eastern terminus of its line from the Pacific Coast; in addition, the Chicago, Rock Island and Pacific, the Missouri Pacific, and the Chicago, Burlington and Quincy also ran to the city.

While Judge Otis and his cronies were busy exercising their civic powers, Mrs. Otis occupied herself with afternoon teas and calls on her neighbors. She had beautiful dark eyes under wavy hair which dipped over her forehead, and her manner was always gentle. Often she wore a black lace dress when she set out in the carriage on her rounds. In 1799 her mother, Maria Grace, had seen George Washington in person in Philadelphia, and her daughter and granddaughter would one day fly across the continent in an airplane. Together Alfred and Amelia Otis symbolized a historical continuity from the American Revolution into the twentieth century.

The couple had eight children, of whom only four survived to old age; Amy was fourth in line. She had her mother's intent dark eyes and dark hair, and her face was long and narrow. She was thin and taller than average, and in later years would appear gaunt. Obviously well-bred, she was amiable for the most part, strong-willed on occasion, gallant in adversity. As a young girl she had been carefree and healthy, kneeling at church in a ruby silk dress, attending balls at Fort Leavenworth, and visiting freely in the house next door with her ten cousins, children of Dr. Paul Challiss and his wife Mary, who was Amelia Harres Otis's sister.

Amy was a leader among young people of Atchison who shared common experiences in growing up together, attending the same private school, and observing the same formalities and traditions of society as their upperclass parents. A good horsewoman and popular dancer, she often participated in political discussions with her father's influential friends. She was intelligent, cultured, interested in books, art, and music. Her hearing had been impaired when she was sixteen in an attack of typhoid fever, and later in life she was dependent on a hearing aid. In 1889, when she was nineteen and preparing to attend Vassar, she was stricken with diphtheria. Nursed by her ninety-two-year-old Grandmother Harres, she finally recovered after a long convalescence. She decided against entering college, and instead went with her father on business trips to the territories of Utah and what later became Oklahoma. In the summer of 1890, when father and daughter were in Colorado, Amy became the first woman ever to climb the final quarter-mile to the top of Pike's Peak.

The Judge undoubtedly expected his daughter to marry a local scion who would be wealthy by inheritance if not through his own efforts, and above all be conventionally and materially ambitious. On the night of her presentation ball, in 1890, Amy's brother Mark introduced her to his college roommate, Edwin Stanton Earhart, a handsome student from the law school at the University of Kansas in Lawrence. Edwin found they danced well together, and Amy said later, "I liked him right away, and I soon knew he liked me too."

The Otises and the Earharts had never met, although they had arrived in Atchison about the same time. Yet if the Otises symbolized one continuity, the Earharts symbolized another. Edwin's scholarly father, the Reverend David Earhart, was an Evangelical Lutheran missionary, descended from Hessians who migrated to Pennsylvania before the Revolution. His great-uncle John Earhart had died fighting under General Washington.

The Reverend Earhart ministered on Sundays to a scattered congregation of Indians and early settlers, taught school through the week, and managed food for his wife and twelve children by working his own hardscrabble farm which was literally on the other side of the railroad tracks. Often johnnycake and turnips provided the family's main meal. He greatly hoped that his youngest child, Edwin, would become a churchman. After graduating from Thiel College in Pennsylvania at eighteen, however, the young man decided on the law as a profession. He worked his way through the University of Kansas by shining shoes, tending furnaces, and tutoring his classmates.

This son of a sod-busting itinerant minister was the man with whom Amy Otis elected to share her future. He was presentable enough, amiable and charming, imaginative, a lover of books, drama, and music, with ability in mathematics and languages; but he lacked social ambition, aggressive determination, and the ruthless drive to send him to a judicial appointment of any distinction.

Distraught and dismayed, Judge Otis soon disrupted the romantic plans of the young couple. For five years he withheld permission for the marriage, insisting that Edwin must be earning at least fifty dollars a month before he would entrust his daughter to so uncertain a prospect. Amy, as stubborn as her father, withstood all efforts to change her mind, and Edwin, after his graduation in 1894, went to work settling claims on a fee basis for the Rock Island and other railroads — for an average of fifty dollars a month.

A small wedding took place on October 16, 1895, and forgoing a reception and honeymoon, the couple went directly to their first home, a house in Kansas City fully furnished and paid for by the bride's father. For twenty-five-year-old Amy, the transition was painful. Her husband was often away on business, she was unused to housework, and she missed the company of her Challiss cousins and other friends in Atchison. She often wept alone and went frequently to visit her parents. Her unhappiness deepened seriously in the following year after an accident caused the stillbirth of her first child, a girl.

When they learned of Amy's second pregnancy, Judge and Mrs. Otis insisted that she come home to bear their grandchild. So it was that Amelia Mary, named for her two grandmothers, was born on July 24, 1897, in Atchison, in the house on Quality Hill. Amy wrote later that the baby was an "eight and a half pounder whose weight was not due to excess fat because her bones were small and nicely covered. She was already tall with a beautifully shaped head and nice hands, a real water color baby with the bluest of blue eyes, rosy cheeks and red lips..."

From her Otis ancestors, Amelia inherited a strong will, grim determination, and a tough sense of Yankee thrift which endowed her with an intelligent, though never ungenerous, respect for money, a virtue that she believed eluded both her parents and her sister. From the Earharts she acquired the imagination of her improvident father, a love of sports and games, music and poetry, and the fervent vision which made her fix on flying to express her deepest compulsions.

When she was growing up, she wrote later, "People just flew in anything which would get off the ground." Any notion of aviation's ever offering a practical career for women was unheard of. A few women had defied the conventions and gravity; a French baroness in 1910 was the first woman to be issued a pilot's license, while Harriet Quimby, an American, qualified in the United States in 1911. Aspirations in others were mostly forbidden by family, or subdued for lack of courage or imagination by the women themselves.

In 1908, when she was eleven years old, Amelia Earhart saw her first airplane at the Iowa State Fair and regarded it with indifference. Years later, at the Exposition in Toronto, she watched with pleasurable fright as a stunt flyer dived toward where she stood on the field. From then on she was obsessed by airplanes, and concomitantly by aviation itself.

First Amelia had a child's life to live, however, and many were the girlhood stories dredged up later to create the public version of a little girl unusually interested in mechanical experimentation, stories which assigned to her everything from making a "rolly coaster" and screaming "It's just like flying," to a strong determination to liberate girls and women from the confines of convention and put them on an equal footing with boys and men. Most of the stories were true, if embellished and overly sentimental, and she obediently contributed to the publicity by recalling others. More frequently she referred to her youth as growing up much as any other American girl.

In reality part of her early life was painfully different from the average. The financial and emotional strain between her parents, though never mentioned directly, arose because Edwin's income depended on settling claims against the railroad for a fee. He was tireless, enthusiastic and desperately sincere, but money was always uncertain and always insufficient. Full of stubborn pride and genuine love for her husband, Amy often accompanied him on his travels. For this reason, the family lived modestly together in Kansas City during the summer months, but Millie and Pidge, as Muriel was called in the family, spent the winters with their doting and extravagant Otis grandparents in Atchison. From the beginning Amelia was shuttled from genteel poverty to wealthy indulgence and back again.

Self-conscious in the bloomers their mother was persuaded by her sister, a devotee of Mrs. Bloomer, to put on them when all other little girls wore long dresses, with their hair braided in pigtails and huge bows over the ears, the sisters attended the private College Preparatory School in Atchison. On weekends and holidays they played games with their cousins and young friends, held mudfights, went on picnics, and explored the sandstone caves on the bluff over the river.

Scorning dolls, Amelia preferred a wooden donkey for taking to bed, and Muriel had an elephant. Mostly their play was directed by surplus energy and wild fantasy. Given a lawn swing, they turned it into a kind of jungle gym, and hung by their knees over the upright bar, heads dangling. Given a primitive merry-go-round, they ran their legs off to gain momentum, and then jumped on to ride until "she died." In the dusty old barn stood a two-seater carriage, no longer used. With their friends, the sisters whipped up nonexistent horses, fought off nonexistent wolves, and screamed themselves hoarse on a journey to "Cherryville," where they never arrived. When it was too hot to play outside, they lay on their stomachs to read bound volumes of *The Youth's Companion, Puck, Harper's Weekly,* or *Harper's Young People,* in time graduating to Victor Hugo, Alexandre Dumas, *père* and *fils,* Charles Dickens, and Oliver Optic's success stories for boys. One Christmas they received sleds and, what was worse to Grandmother Otis, a .22-caliber Hamilton rifle. Amelia was nine years old and wanted to rid the barn of rats.

Occasionally their father, with increasing sensitivity to Otis condescension, would arrive to take them fishing; or he and Amelia would sit at the piano "composing." Both played by ear, and in time she would join the Mandolin Club at Ogontz. Still later, living in Northampton with her sister, she spent half the money set aside to buy coal on a secondhand banjo. Sometimes their mother retired to Atchison for a rest from the carefully concealed tension of her marriage.

In 1907 Edwin transferred to the claims department of the Rock Island Railroad, where he was put on salary, and Amelia and Muriel spent one last year with their grandparents while Amy hunted for a suitable house in Des Moines, Iowa. In 1908 Amelia and Muriel went to live permanently in their own home with their own loving and beloved parents. Neither had any reason to believe a carefree and secure existence would not continue. The move was, however, a watershed in their lives: a long period of misery and suffering was about to begin.

THREE

Family Secret
1908-1916

At first in Des Moines the Earhart family enjoyed being together. Amy had learned to cook, and once when she was cutting up a chicken, she pointed out the anatomical wonder of lungs fitted into the cavity above the heart, and how the wings were jointed as in the human wrist. She sewed for herself and taught her daughters to make, or make over, their own clothes; neither enjoyed the task. In the evenings Edwin read aloud or told marvelous stories, and one night he insisted the children be allowed to stay up until eleven o'clock to watch an eclipse of the moon. On Saturdays he played Indian Wars with the girls and any neighbor children who came to join the fun. He was prospering to an extent he never would again, having in one year been advanced to the position of chief of the Rock Island claims department.

Naturally Millie and Pidge found some differences in their new life. Their playmates were all back in Atchison, and they could not run freely on city streets as they had on Quality Hill. For the first year they were tutored at home, Amy rejecting public school for the grandchildren of Judge Otis. In the end, however, she was forced to give way; twenty-five dollars a month was too hard on the family budget, even though Edwin's salary recently had been doubled. Being of fundamentally sensible disposition despite her scale of values and standards, she may also have realized that her daughters needed competition and companionship. She enrolled them in the nearest public school.

Edwin still traveled widely, sometimes in a private car which allowed him to take his family along on trips as far away as California. At such times Amy would request advance assignments from the school so the girls would not drop behind in their studies. Both were good scholars, although their interests differed: Muriel developed a passion for English and literature, Amelia preferred physics and mathematics. All the family loved books. Often the housework was done as one or another of them read aloud a novel by Scott, Dickens, George Eliot, or Thackeray.

For several summers the Earharts went to Worthington on Lake Okabena in Minnesota, boarding at a home where the sisters learned to ride, with or without a saddle, helped milk the cows, went fishing, played tennis, and in time danced in the evenings to "Alexander's Ragtime Band" or "Red Wing" played on a wind-up Victrola.

Until 1910 the undertow which was insidiously pulling the family down to destruction was only mentioned as "Dad's sickness." Edwin, who had been happiest when he was working independently on a fee basis, had succumbed to boredom on a salary. He began to drink. For some years he more and more often failed to keep business engagements, neglected his work, emotionally wounded his wife and daughters, and finally suffered a "general nervous breakdown," as his family called it. Amy and the two girls fiercely guarded their tongues in public and clung together in private.

As a result, Amelia suffered a deep and probably unrecognized, certainly an unacknowledged, sense of guilt. On an occasion when she seized a bottle and poured the whiskey down the sink, Edwin saw her and was only just prevented from striking her. The effects on a loving and sensitive thirteen-year-old were traumatic: recoil in disbelief at the violent action of a usually loving and indulgent parent, and the stunning realization that she was absolutely without power to alter her father's behavior, either toward drinking or toward violence to her or anyone, when he was under the control of alcohol.

As the older child Amelia became overly protective of her mother and sister, an attitude she never lost, and one which in the future would sometimes make her appear domineering and arrogant in her relation to them. Maturity would later bring understanding of her father's illness, however, and in 1930, after his death, she wrote her mother, "He asked about you and Pidge a lot, and I faked telegrams for him from you all. He was an aristocrat as he went — the weaknesses gone, with a little boy's brown puzzled eyes." She paid all his bills and was with him almost to the moment of his death. Furthermore, although she herself never touched alcohol, she did not withdraw from the 1928 transatlantic flight when she discovered the pilot had a drinking problem, nor flinch in 1937 from choosing a recovered alcoholic to be her navigator for the fatal world flight.

At thirteen, however, afraid to trust her own feelings about the family misery, Amelia had little sympathy when Edwin was dismissed by his employer. He was persuaded after some effort to spend a month "taking the cure," from which he returned under solemn oath never again to "take another drop" now that he was all "cleaned up inside." Undoubtedly he meant what he said, but his mother-in-law's final illness, which began in 1910, precipitated a catastrophe from which neither he nor the family ever fully recovered.

Judge Otis was already dead, and Amy was perhaps secretly relieved to remove herself to Atchison and with her sister, Margaret Balis, attend their mortally ill mother. Millie and Pidge remained in Des Moines with their father, and Amelia at fourteen coped responsibly with minor family crises while her mother was away. Mrs. Otis's death affected her deeply because she had been her grandmother's favorite; but according to Amy she didn't speak much of her grief, burying it inside as she did all deep emotion.

Unfortunately Mrs. Otis had heard of her son-in-law's "sickness," and after her death in September of 1911, her will directed that her fortune of close to a half-million dollars be divided equally among her four surviving children, with Amy's share to be put in trust for twenty years — or until Edwin Earhart was dead. This cruelty completed Edwin's humiliation by the Otises. His drinking became incessant, his conduct intolerable. The family was unevenly divided and totally unhappy.

Nor did the situation basically improve when in 1913 Edwin went to work as a freight clerk for the Great Northern Railway, and the Earharts moved to St. Paul, Minnesota. His salary took care of the rent, but the income from Amy's inheritance was required for all other expenses. Night after night Edwin arrived home drunk, until the night he staggered into the path of an automobile and did not come home at all. Although not badly hurt, he was briefly hospitalized and he lost his job. Offered a better one with the Chicago, Burlington and Quincy Railroad in Springfield, Missouri, he moved the family yet again, only to find the employee he was to replace had changed his mind about retiring. There was no job, there was no offer of a job.

Temporarily the family was forced to break up. Edwin went to Kansas City, where he lived with his sister and her family, and, denied further railroad employment because of his reputation, opened his own law office. Amy accepted the charitable hospitality of the Shedd family, old friends from Kansas City, and took the girls to live in Chicago.

Amelia, bent on the best scientific education she could get, entered Hyde Park High School, and won the despairing respect of her teachers. She was brilliant, quickly mastering whatever she set her mind to, but she refused to explain how she arrived at the correct answers to complex mathematical or scientific problems. *She* knew how she got her answers, and she was certain her teachers knew that she knew. To explain the obvious was only a waste of time.

Whatever her responsibilities, whatever her private anxieties and griefs, Amelia did not discuss them. Neither did she let them dim her spirit. After still another family move, she wrote from St. Paul to Virginia Park, a school friend in Atchison:

[March 6, 1914]

Blessings on thee, Little Ginger —

...Of course I'm going to B.M. [Bryn Mawr] if I have to drive a grocery wagon to accumulate the cash. You see I'm practicing grocery boy language because if I use up all my money going to hear grand "Hopery" why — I'll be minus later that's all. I wish you were up here because Parsifal and I don't know what are coming here. I suppose they will be in K.C. [Kansas City] I'm all thrills. Did you hear Paderewski...I wonder if he played Chopin Funeral March down at St. Joe as he did here.

You miss much by not having Gym. Last Fri. we had a circus. We played B.B. [basketball] just like you and I did once upon a time (remember) No boys tho. I don't know when I've been so tired.

All the girls are so nice it's a joy to be with them don't you know. I am doing my best to get some of them to go to B.M. with Ginger and Millie.

Your letter was scrummy. So long and joysome. I'll send you the translation of your Cicero. I'm a shark ...Your letter was very funny. I lawffed ex'cessively.

Speaking of funny things, my dear freshman of a sister spoke very importantly of "forum" in their class meeting (All those lambs attend their meeting religiously) completely mystifying the family until mother had the happy thot she meant quorum...

It's so hot today I am just baked. I want this reading matter to go off on the next mail so I'll cease.

Love, Mill.

I'll write you a sensible letter someday. You needn't ans. this communication unless you have nothing else to do. All contributions, however, are thankfully received at this end.

In her private correspondence, Amelia delighted in mangling words, making obvious grammatical errors, and using abbreviations and initials in a style peculiarly her own, but she was as correct and graceful in formal letters as she was in published articles. In her flight records she sometimes combined the two styles, as in this excerpt from the log she kept of the *Friendship* flight in 1928. "...There is nothing to see but churned mist, very white in the afternoon sun...I have et a orange..."

When her mother was living in "Bean Town" (Boston) or on vacation at "Miggleshead" (Marblehead), Massachusetts, Amelia sent her "lil sprizes for Chrismuzz," and at times she was "remisser" than usual in sending her mother's "keck" which was a "dol or more short" once in a while. *She* knew how to spell and punctuate correctly, and she was confident her reader would know she knew, so why not have a little fun?

After Amelia's graduation from Hyde Park High School in June of 1915, Amelia, her mother and sister joined Edwin in Kansas City, where he was working independently as a lawyer and no longer drinking. Although his family relationships would never recover fully, he could and did triumph over the ugly Otis influence by persuading his reluctant wife to break her mother's will. The trust on which survival for the Earharts almost literally depended was being mismanaged and had lost a good deal of money in the hands of Amy's brother Mark. Supported by testimony from her mother's doctor, Amy won a dissolution of the trust, and the remaining principal, approximately $60,000, was turned over to her.

With money in hand, Amy elected first to send her daughters away to school in the fall of 1916. She wanted Muriel to have some British and Canadian teachers, so as a freshman her younger daughter entered St. Margaret's College in the Canadian city of Toronto. Amelia, having filed too late for admission to Vassar, chose the Ogontz School. Near Philadelphia, this "female college" had associations for the Earhart family, since as early as 1895, the year of Amy's marriage, a distant relative had been a teacher there, and Amy may herself have attended there at one time. Amelia was nineteen, slim and intense, more often frowning than smiling, a fine scholar, and an introvert subject to conflicting emotions generated by her stubborn opposition to certain conventions of society and habits of the family. Some of these were too deep for recognition; all had great influence on her attitudes and actions in the future. She accepted as a matter of course the theory that in order to keep one's place in the social order one followed ongoing traditions, but individual honor, integrity, loyalty, and responsibility were instinctive.

On the other hand, many of society's strictures were inimical to her sense of independence, thirst for innovation, and feminism. As a small tomboy, she had offended Grandma Otis with her behavior, romping around Quality Hill, jumping the fence instead of using the gate; Grandma had irritated her by trying to make her into a proper little lady. While by birth and breeding Amelia would always be a lady in the social sense, the imposition of what she considered purely artificial distinctions between the sexes would always disturb her sense of justice. Her desire for feminine equality was as insistent as her interest in aviation, and eventually her enthusiastic promotion of one always included and emphasized the other.

Living together as a family had once been happy and serene, but Amelia was now glad to leave behind the parental disharmony, which at one time she was certain she had caused by something done or not done, she couldn't guess what. Now she knew better. She had not been able to stop her father's drinking any more than she could prevent her parents' unhappiness. Faced with this reality, she may have determined never to get so close that failing another person would be the same as failing herself.

Going away to school would separate Amelia from her parents, and also from sister Muriel. In their childhood Amelia had led the fun at Quality Hill in Atchison, always ready with a new game before the old one became boring. Muriel went along, proud of her sister and happy at her ability to stimulate amusements for the ten Challiss cousins as well as herself. After the move to Kansas City, however, the sisters had to depend on each other for companionship. They had gone to school at home, which marked them as different from neighbor children, and later when their father's drinking made life almost unbearable, they were preoccupied in consoling themselves and Amy while making sure no hint of the family unhappiness escaped from the house. Muriel was then less competitive with than emulative of Amelia — an attitude never displaced in later years, when she would strenuously deny any question of unfriendly rivalry between them.

The time came when trunks were packed and trains departed, one to Toronto, where Amy settled Muriel in school, and later one to Philadelphia, where Amy took Amelia. The extended absence from the family led to a series of letters invariably directed to Mrs. Earhart, possibly because Amelia was closer to her mother, or because her father's traveling schedule made addressing him difficult, or both. She did not, and never would, feel easy about Edwin again, nor quite the same about Amy.

Fortunately several of these school letters have survived, and they reveal a side of Amelia Earhart which both she and the public legend failed entirely to develop.

FOUR

Boarding School 1916-1917

The Ogontz School was located in wooded hilly country on what is now a campus of the Pennsylvania State University a short distance north of Philadelphia. It was exclusive, most students coming from upper-middle-class families, and heavily endowed, boasting a fine art gallery and funds for lectures by noted men of letters. The headmistress was conservative and conventional Miss Abby Sutherland who in later years would remember Amelia as "always pushing into unknown seas in her reading." The girl's poise, reserve and curiosity were characteristics that appealed to the headmistress, whom at first Amelia described as "come up from the depths."

Not even Amelia ever publicly filled in the eighteen months she attended Ogontz, and in fact little if any published reference was ever made anywhere to the influence the school had on her, or she on it. Yet her letters reveal a boarding school experience which not only crystallized her independence and added to her maturity, but for a girl was far in advance of the social climate of the time.

School records show that she entered Ogontz on October 3, 1916. She was in attendance during 1917 and the spring of 1918. Her tuition and board came to $600 a half year, and she went on chaperoned excursions into Philadelphia to attend concerts and opera. These were charged to her account along with text-

25

books and such other incidentals as medicine (10¢) and even postage (12¢).

Her letters home were directed to Mrs. Earhart at the house on Charlotte Street and later to the Hotel Sutherland, both in Kansas City. In the fall of 1917, Mrs. Earhart went to stay at the St. Regis, an apartment hotel in Toronto. While their daughters were away at school, Amy and Edwin were moving toward a separation.

Although Amelia's letters say almost nothing directly about United States participation in World War I, they do record her patriotic efforts as well as her comments on the family situation, her attitude toward academic authority, and her relations with her fellow students.

Ogontz, [October 25, 1916]

Dearest Mother:

I have been so busy I haven't had time to do anything for myself much less anything for my family, like writing them letters. This is a small minute of time snatched before church-time and getting one of the girls [Leonora Hassinger] ready to go in an hour, her trunk I mean. She is so nice and reminds me of Toot [Lucy Challiss, a cousin] at least the Toot I used to know...She and I have grown so fond of each other. She was graduated two years ago and comes back every so often because she is a great friend of Miss Sutherland and her younger sister is in the room right out of ours. They are of a very fine family, the Hassingers of Birmingham. They come from New Orleans and Leonora is going to make her debut there this winter altho she has been presented in Birmingham. She leaves tomorrow with her father for New York where he has business and she may stay over and visit. I may be able to go and visit her for one night and day at the Waldorf and do some shopping as none of us has gone in town and Miss Sutherland doesn't feel safe about it. She says she knows the food we get here is good as she supervises it herself but she doesn't know what we might get in town and she doesn't want any sick people on her hands.

She is a very brilliant woman, very impressive as she is taller than I and large. When I first saw her I thot she was come up from the depths as her cheek bones are high and her face seemed hard somehow.

I went into the Philadelphia Symphony Concert a week ago. There were five and Miss Sutherland and we went in her car, and she was so charming that I can't feel my first impression [was correct] altho I have watched her closely. She has had many chances of matrimony because she is brilliant but she passes them all by. She has read very widely and has very good ideas about lots of things but she's pro-Wilson [Thomas Woodrow Wilson, President 1913–1920] I think. We have current events every Saturday morning, an address on current times by Miss Sutherland and I gather from that she is for him as is most of the east.

I played hockey yesterday and made two goals, the only ones made. It has been so rainy that we haven't been able to play basketball or anything. Drill is awful. I look like a broomstick wrapped round and round. [A sketch shows her very tall and thin with wide shoulders and a narrow waist; her suit has a long-sleeved jacket, buttoned down the front, and a pleated skirt.] Thus nearly everybody looks awful. But I worst. I can wear an old suit with a little alteration so it will be more reasonable. I hate to spend money for things I never will need nor want. I bot a pair of Leonora's black high-heeled slippers. They fit me and I needed some and she didn't like them so I bot them for five dollars. They were seven and she had only worn them since Wednesday a week ago.

You will "pop" when I tell you about a drawing room evening we had last Thursday. Miss Pughsey's evening they call it. She has us walk bow sit stand shake hands etc. etc. My law. I was at the end of the line by chance and she spotted me first. So *I* had to come out and perform before everyone *first*. Shake hands etc. The funniest thing was the sitting. She put a little chair out in the middle of this huge room and we all aimed at it and tried to *clammer* on it gracefully. It was a scream. One of the girls landed with her legs crossed, on the extreme edge. I got on but not with noticeable grace as there was no comment made.

I am continuing this letter Monday evening. I played Hockey again to-day and made a goal thru my legs which convulsed on-lookers. In the midst of the game a telephone call for me came which was cousin Annie [Balis?]. Jane [a Balis cousin] is better and they will be in quarantine until the middle of November. Uncle Clarence [Balis, married to Amy's sister Margaret] stays away from the house so he can attend to business.

Everything is beautiful here. The trees and wild-flowers are splotches of color and the green hasn't faded from the grass yet.

Did I tell you I have a reputation for brains? So much so that I am taking third French. We read George Sands' [sic] "The Devil's Pool." I don't have a minute for anything because I want to get all possible.

Weekdays this is the program.

7:00 Get up to a cow bell.

7:30 Prayers and afterward setting up exercises.

8:00 Breakfast and morning walk till school begins at nine. Classes until two. One fifteen in my case. Then Hockey, b.ball or drill in turn with an hour or two for tennis.

4 to 5:30 Study hall

5:30 — 6:30 Dress for dinner

6:00 Dinner and prayers immediately after. Then spelling. Then every evening we have something to do. Thursday and Tuesday conversation classes in French German etc. Wednesday a lecture or something like that (Joseph Hoffmann this Wednesday) and Friday always something else. Saturday and Monday are our free nights. Sunday prayers and a lecture take up the time. Saturday Current Events. Bible, Art, take up the time till luncheon. Then everybody takes two hours of exercise out-doors. Then Study at four as usual. You see every minute is accounted for and you have to go by schedule.

I never shall get this letter off if I don't close now as this is Wednesday morning and it was begun Sunday.

Lots of love,
Mill

Ogontz, [March, 1917]

Dearest Mother:

Today is a wet rainy gray day and most every body has been in the building all the time. Only a few brave souls went out, I among them, for a walk, but we were fully repaid for our bravery as it was splendid to have the wind blow and the rain beat in your face.

So many things have happened since my last epistle. In the first place as I think I told you Charles R. Kennedy read his "Terrible Meek" to us. Last night the Orpheus Club, a musical organization of Philadelphia, composed of about twenty men aged from twenty-five to eighty, came out to dinner here and gave us a concert. There were some magnificent voices caged in very unprepossessing exteriors and one German Baron looked as tho he would burst his earthly shell when he sang, but his voice was a wonderfully clear barytone. He sung from Fauré and Die Walkyrie (I know how to spell it). It is not a club that gives public entertainment but there are many connections with Ogontz and they get a rather good meal so they come out annually for our gratification.

We had a lovely feast the other night. There were about fifteen of us and several teachers were away so that it was a lovely opportunity. We played the ukuleles at twelve o'clock and sang and no one will believe it. Some of the girls had been away and brot back chicken sandwiches and cakes and pastry and we made hot chocolate and put marshmallow on it and had a beautiful time. Drank it out of trophy cups. Also ice cream.

Tonight is the camera club dance and St. Patrick's dinner combined. Very festive I imagine.

What do you think of the railroad strike and the abdication of the Tzar [Nicholas II of Russia]? There seems to be no public sentiment back of the unions as there was in the beginning which will make their demands harder of attainment. They have gone too far.

Dearie, I don't need any spring clothes so don't worry about sending me money. I have a few dollars still in the bank and I know you all need things more than I. Will I stay here at Auntie's for Easter vacation? providing she [Margaret Otis Balis, Amy's sister] asks me over. Don't, don't have a thot about me as I am getting along alright with things as they are. I only need worry over you all — especially if you send any money as I know some things you will *have* to do.

Affectionately
A.

When the Ogontz School closed for the summer of 1917, Amelia may have gone directly home, or she may have visited relatives or friends en route. She was apparently in Kansas City in late July and then traveled as far as Chicago accompanied by her father, on her way for a vacation with young friends at Camp Gray on the eastern shore of Lake Michigan.

Chicago, [July 31, 1917]

Dearest Mom,

I have been here for about forty-five minutes... checking my baggage and buying a ticket to Holland

[Michigan] which is $3.91. Pete said Sarah left at six this morning. As we found I leave at noon. The trip here was lovely as far as service etc was concerned but I never was on such a beastly dirty trip in my life. I scrubbed my face and neck so hard it looks as tho I had hives. I am going to try and call the Shedds and will send this off immediately so you may know how things are so far.

Poppy was such a lamb last night I came near coming back with him.

L.O.L.
Amelia

Holland, on an inlet of Lake Michigan, at that time was reached either by railroad or boat from Chicago. Camp Gray was at Saugatuck, approximately twenty miles south of Holland, on the lakeshore at the mouth of the Kalamazoo River. The town was small, and conditions were primitive, no electricity or hot water, but Amelia for the first time in her twenty years began to enjoy the friendship and attention of young men her own age. Always before her social contacts had been with groups of boys and girls, many of them cousins, who trooped into the Earhart kitchen to make fudge or pull taffy, groups at high school or church, and at neighborhood parties to which her father or mother took her and called to escort her home. Not only were opportunities limited, any special interest she might have had in boys was retarded by the social conventions of the time. Now all that changed.

Camp Gray, [August 1, 1917]

Dearest Mater,

I surely have had a wildly exciting time and don't send Pidge without wiring for accommodations as there is not a vacant place. I will see what I can do today.

Mother, Sarah is not here yet! When in Chicago I called Pete and he said she had left at six o'clock. Well, they just took off the day boats, the route she told Mrs. Merrill she intended to take, and she evidently will get in this morning instead of last night as expected.

However I arrived then and had a dreadful time finding my way. I thot it most peculiar not to be met etc. and fortunately met the camp Major-domo, who escorted me over. Very thankful to be under his protection. Well, reached here and bumped (figuratively) into Mr. Merrill at the desk. He flew out and came back with Mrs. Merrill who just was *lovely*. We are in one of her rooms. Her daughter's who is in Vermont, the only vacant room on the place.

Ken is here and took me immediately to play in the sand and walk on the beach a delightful experience despite high heels and a tendency to be as quiet as possible which came upon me in Chicago — much to my joy as I can go in swimming in a day or two for the rest of the time.

Things are rather primitive but the waitresses are all college girls working their way thru. I have just had breakfast, and while not elegant very good for camp.

We are all going over for Sarah so must end this to mail.

L.O.L.
Amelia

Camp Gray, [August 8, 1917]

Dearest Mother,

Since I have heard "garnichts" from you since arriving I am snatching a few moments from a rather full day to tell you much. Under no circumstances could K. [possibly Katchie Challiss, a cousin] and Muriel come up without you. There is not a place and it is impossible to be alone. Sarah and I would be lost without the Merrills, as Mrs. Merrill has been kindness itself and Ken has toted me around considerably.

I am in mental torture at not going in swimming and

imagine I am thot of as somewhat of a piker — that way anyway. Things are very primitive and the food is not very good, however probably conducive to rugged health it may be, tho I have my doubts about the nutritive value of oleomargarine. The only desirable qualities are the climate and scenery and I am having a wonderful time just being with Sarah. I should never choose it as a ideal place without friends to make one overlook lack of hot water, oil lamps, etc.

The mail is going out and I want this to go.

L.O.L.

A.

Camp Gray, [August 14, 1917]
Dearest Mother,

Your selfish and guilty feeling daughter is coming home. I can't stand it any longer and especially as Sarah could, but does not feel as tho she ought to stay longer we will both leave tomorrow, Wednesday the fifteenth. I have enough money to get to Chicago after paying board at only $9.80 per week and as Kenneth and Harry left day before yesterday and have planned opera and baseball games etc. for a few days I said I thot you would let me stay at Mr. Tredwell's after their strong invitation.

The boys have been lovely and Kenneth has done so much for me. He is very nice and sensitive and almost brilliant. We four have just ideal times together and have gone on innumerable canoe trips, walking jaunts etc. together. I can't think of hot weather since it is almost too chilly for comfort but I can not bear to be so privileged...[Mrs. Merrill] is a dear and has been so brave thru so many many trials. Her oldest son just wired [he] is awaiting a hoped for commission; her middle son is going and her daughter is very ill besides lots of other things. I'll have loads to tell you when I see you.

Affectionately
Amelia

Camp Gray, [August 15, 1917]

Dear Maw,

Received word last evening that Mrs. Tredwell was not well and was going to the hospital for a few days to take radium treatments. Mr. Tredwell urged me to come however if I would not mind being quiet but of course I declined and will stay here until I can come home as per my preceding letter. In case this reaches you first...Harry and Ken were going to take us to everything in Chicago this weekend...They are such nice boys and we have had a wonderful time with them.

I can stay here indefinitely except for the fact that Ken will come up to see me over the week end and without Sarah I should not feel quite comfortable — it seeming as tho I might possibly be waiting for him and doing it purposely. However if it is inconvenient to have me home I will gladly stay.

There are several very nice girls of about fifteen or so and a small group of older women and one boy of twenty-three who is exceptionally fine and who has been very nice to me whenever he could. He is an old family friend of the Tredwells and he and his mother are here for a while longer. I like her so much. His father was on Roosevelt's personal Rough Rider staff and was very well known. Gordon Pollack is his name. He is very interested in photography and was offered a position as war photographer but refused it to go into the aviation corps. He has made several dozen studies of *me* which I am anxious to see and which I hope will be good.

I want this to go out on the same train.

Affectionately
Amelia

Presumably, she did return to spend the rest of the summer with her family. In October she registered as a senior at the Ogontz School, which had moved to a new location near the Huntington Valley Club.

FIVE

Wartime Nurse's Aide 1917–1918

Mrs. Earhart when later asked if Amelia ever questioned her judgment replied, "...undoubtedly in her heart sometimes she would question my judgment but never...up to the time she was nineteen or twenty...Then she would say every once in a while 'I don't agree with you at all, Mother. This is the way I look at it,' but she was frank and we would talk about it."

Amelia was twenty when she returned to the Ogontz School in October 1917. Her long thin body had assumed pleasing adult lines, although her blue eyes remained as direct and uncompromising as a child's. Her inner ear was still finely tuned to the "silent severity" of the temporary separation between her parents which was about to take place, or perhaps already had, because during the fall and over Christmas Mrs. Earhart had resided at the St. Regis.

Steaming with energy and idealism, Amelia plunged into school activities, knitted for the American Red Cross, studied and went on excursions as she had the year before, but with a difference. Whether from repeated clashes with academic authority, from overdoing, as her mother suspected, or because of certain character traits, Amelia was a loner, by choice. In her high school yearbook, the caption under her photograph read, "The girl in brown who walks alone." The condition was permanent, and now she found herself in discord with her associates and with Ogontz itself.

Ogontz, [October, 1917]

Dear Mammy,

'Tis some time since I last wrote you, but as usual I have had a very busy time. We have had much revolution in school. It is a different place entirely. Miss Sutherland has abolished sororities completely sans any hope, I believe, of return. It is a sweeping blow and only one who has seen them in action knows how tremendous it is. She has instituted in the same breathless iconoclastic measure the honor system which will I imagine stop all surreptitious student activities.

We have seventy-six new girls and only about thirty-nine old ones. There are some fine specimens among the new girls and I have every hope of another Ogontz just as good to arise from the ruins of the old order. I always arrive at the climax of everything, don't I? However our class est composé of splendid girls tho not so impressive in numbers as last year's.

I have a very nice roommate [Eleanor Hoover] and we get on splendidly.

The general age of the school is older perhaps because the young girls are over at another house, but whatever it is, I am much more satisfied. The building is wonderful and tho not ready in every respect can take care of us at any rate. The swimming pool is not filled yet and the hockey field not finished. That is all.

Miss Sutherland has taken a beautiful estate for the smaller school, fourteen and fifteen year olds, not far from here. It is magnificently situated and it is an education and inspiration to live in it. Then there is the graduate house which is owned by Miss S. and is very lovely. The country here is superb and the gorgeousness of autumnal coloring is almost too much. We are in the vicinity of Huntington Valley Club and can see the golfers playing on the beautiful course from our top windows.

I have awful twinges of conscience about leaving you to your silent severity (your description). I knew exactly what you were going to have to endure and feel as tho I could have alleviated some of the loneliness had I remained faithful to my intentions.

I had a nice letter from de Poppy and he enclosed stamps. I wrote Detroit to forward mail here so I am enclosing the fruit of my thotfulness.

I must dress for dinner soon but will write you before long again.

Affectionately
Amelia

Ogontz, October 16 [?], 1917

Dearest Mother,

I began a letter to you several days ago but cannot now find it. I have been so busy with the course I am taking and the offices the girls have voted me into. I am Vice President of the class which entails several unusual privileges such as the trip to New York Miss Sutherland always gives the senior officers and many others. Then I am secretary by popular vote to a Red Cross Chapter we are organizing and Eleanor Hoover with whom I am now rooming is chairman. She is a wonder and I think I am envied more than anyone in having her as a roommate.

Then I am secretary and treasurer of Christian Endeavor — no sinecure. It has been rather an institution of torture heretofore, and not well liked but we are trying to put something into it that will make it stand for something.

I am trying to manage to attend Cousin Annie's wedding tomorrow night. I want to very much but don't know whether I can or not.

I am taking Modern Drama Literature, German and German Literature outside. French three and five in which latter we are reading Eugénie Grandet. And Senior arithmetic and logic if I can. Besides reading a good deal and art, Bible, etc. etc.

I am elected too to write the senior song, but you know the more one does the more one can do. I am very glad I came back and only hope I can get as much from this year's work as I should to repay you for the sacrifice and to justify my return. I am trying mightily.

I received the twenty dollars and as yet have not broken it as my expenses have gone on the house bill so far. Cap and gown etc. I was very glad to have it. All for now.

Affectionately,
Amelia

Ogontz, [October, 1917]

Dear Mammy —

Your letter reached here this morning — and the clippings. Thank you for sending them. Despite my unusual activity I am very well organized to do more the more I do. You know what I mean.

Dear hen, don't write Miss S. letters of advice and warning. They go thru the whole faculty and come to me and I just shrivel. I am not overdoing and all that is needed to bouncing health is plenty to eat and happiness. Consider me bursting, please.

Things are getting into running shape here and going much more smoothly. We wear our caps and gowns on Halloween for the first time. Great day. Our color is green and our flower the gardenia and class motiv "Honor is the foundation of courage" in Latin. Assembled by me in appropriate expression of the institution of the honor system and the courage to confess.

I did not get in to the wedding as school authorities *balked* and Aunty was very crowded and various things. I am going in Sunday week I think.

Mother, just think we have knitted up over fifty dollars worth of stuff in three days. Isn't that wonderful? Thank you for the Liberty bonds. I certainly shall be expert in clipping.

How is my dearest little Mumsey getting along? I am rejoiced about the suit. I wish I could see it. I had a letter from Dad substantiating yours which I must answer. He enclosed a picture of Muriel from the star [Kansas City *Star*]. Rah. Rah. I shall write you again soon.

L.O.L.

Amelia

Ogontz, [November, 1917]

Dear Mother,

I have a few moments before going to bed in which to write you a disagreeable letter. Our senior caps and gowns and flowers for Halloween amounted to twenty seven dollars and thirty six cents. They cannot go on the house bill but must be paid in cash of which I have not enough. I can borrow from Miss S. if it is not con-venient to send me some cash soon as is the custom.

I should write you in detail about the installation of the honor system of which I compose some of its board. There are five of us and we have the school under us. Great life being little models etc. Miss S. wanted faculty members on the board but we declined it so she is raging about mob rule and claiming we all are "blackguards," so called and putting every failure to us. We are grubbing to make things go at least this week so she will be more satisfied.

L.O.L.

Amelia

Ogontz, [November, 1917]

Dear Mother,

This is the first Sunday quiet hour we have had for a long while. The Sunday lecturers have been coming at four or thereabout and cutting our afternoon in half. . .

Things are going better as a whole anyway. I imagine I will be here for Thanksgiving as Auntie has not yet written me. There are about twenty who will remain and they are on the whole our crowd and we expect to have rather a bearable time.

I was a little worried when I wrote you last and want now to correct any impression of unhappiness I may have given you. Some of the girls were agitating the reinstatement of sororities after the respective presidents had given Miss S. their word that no such thing should continue, on the ground that they themselves had not promised. It was a blow to me to see some of the girls I thot much of take that absolutely unethical attitude and I certainly landed into some of them for their conduct. We, Alpha Phi, refused to continue in secret and stood out against such procedure. Somehow Miss S. found out about the intrigue and blew up and threatened to expel about twenty girls. Everything has ended — thank goodness. When I wrote I felt as tho I had lost all my friends or a good many for jumping on them so — as very few people understand what I mean when I go at length into the subtleties of moral codes.

How is my dearest Mummy. I am wild to see you and will think of you on Thanksgiving day. About forty of us went in to hear Aida the other evening and it was wonderful. The audience was stunning in consistent evening dress and showing no signs of war stress. Martinelli sang beautifully and the whole opera was almost dazzling in its gorgeousness of staging.

Where will we be Christmas? Already Miss Dennis (power behind the throne) is arranging trains. I am just wild, more than usual, to see my family.

I heard from Harry the other day and he has never received my letter from Detroit . . . Ken is home now and Gord is ready to be shipped off to training camp anytime. I haven't heard from Poppy lately.

Affectionately,
Amelia

P.S. My nickname here is either Meelie or Butterball — butter for short.   A.

Ogontz, [November, 1917]

Dearest Mother,

I have a few moments of leisure and so despite having written you recently will send a few lines. Economy has hit this school. We are bugs on Liberty bonds. Being secretary and treasurer of several things I know the state of tightness of the gouty money market. We are subscribing to Liberty bonds and try to do without everything else we can. Quite hysterical about attending good theaters and overlook entirely the effect of french gray walls continually.

Today is a windy rainy day and Eleanor and I must go to Red Cross headquarters to see about some of that work. It is very fascinating surely and I know for a good cause. There have been distracting rumors of graft floating around and some very specific instances of it in some of the chapters. I wonder if you could send me some of that lovely khaki yarn from there enough for a heavy sweater, five balls on double thread I think. We are going to start surgical dressings as soon as we are able as our bills for wool are running sky high and I can't let Miss Sutherland go bankrupt.

You won't write any more about me to school dearest Mummy will you?

You know we are trying to persuade the members of the class to forgo the extravagance of a class ring — an expensive one at least as has been the custom for years. Gretchen Harbert and a small coterie are sticking fast for a useless costly ring which is valuable only for the metal in it as there is no artistic and long lasting value in a class ring. We others are only asking we turn our money to R.C. and have only a little gold band for a trifle, about four or five dollars instead of the expensive ones — in order to keep its precedent and to have a remembrance of our senior days. Much sweeter to me than a gorgeous one to pass on. I do not know how we will come out...

I had a letter from Tootie [Challiss] saying she had

broken her engagement but not saying why. It was quite a blow to me, as I stuck up for her when the town was talking, etc. She is going out twice as much again, and very cheerful.

Affectionately,
Amelia

Ogontz, [November, 1917]

Dear Mother,

Your letter and check came yesterday and I was very glad to get both. Thank you for the money. It seems unnecessary to pay for our things as no one has any cash and it causes so much inconvenience.

Mother, may I go to the game between Hill School and Hotchkiss next Saturday I think it is, with Eleanor — whose brother is captain of the team? That is the big game of the season and her father will take us there on the train, a two hour ride, and we come back in the evening with him and plan to have dinner in the Bellevue. I just want you to tell me in your next letter that you approve as of course I must have your permission to go. Mr. Hoover is president of a Bank in Washington and I never could describe Eleanor.

Last Friday evening Miss Sutherland took the officers of the class in town to hear Harry Lauder as a special treat. He was very very good and we enjoyed it so much because it was the first time any of us had been allowed outside the door. As I told you Miss S. is mad upon having any vacation at all and makes so much ado over a simple request that one would rather stay at home than face her and be refused.

We were all ready to go to the theater last night and the last minute she said no one but the girls from the West could go, which was only I in the whole party, so our evening's plan was frustrated.

Then I must tell you that we are in the throes of student government and that I am on the governing board. We were elected by the vote of the school and the girls have cooperated very well so far. Miss Sutherland had some favorites she wished on [us] whom no one can abide and who have no influence in the school. She talked about them and said they were splendid girls and had the ability of leaders and I nearly had my head taken off when I told her the essence of true leadership was to have the girls behind you. She says the school is silly not to appreciate them etc.

We are working hard to make a success of things. There will I am sure be an outbreak soon as the girls must have some recreation. We cannot have our Victrolas because it sounds like a "beergarden" to have them. Basket ball isn't started yet etc. In fact Mother we have nothing to do but dance after dinner Saturday and Monday evenings and only a few of us at that because so many did not get out of spelling that it takes sometimes most of the evening to spell. We're getting a deadly monotone kind of french gray souls and will all be prudes or savages soon.

Your letters are so nice and the clippings help me with my editorials which is Senior composition. This letter is certainly lengthening out but there is a good deal to tell you. I am glad Muriel is getting along on her paper so well...

Thank you so much for the wool. Can I knit it and send it back for you to dispose of as I can not turn it in here?

By the way Eleanor and I as befits officers of the A.R.C. are taking a teachers' course in surgical dressings and we will start it here. This is enough for now...

L.O.L.
Amelia

For Christmas Amelia went to Toronto to join her mother and sister, while her father spent the holiday in Kansas City. Having been sequestered at Ogontz from the war, she had not confronted the realities of armed conflict. In Toronto she could not escape them. Later she often recalled how affected she was by the sight of four one-legged men walking as best they could down King Street, and how she saw no glory, but only the results of a desperate struggle, "men without arms and legs, men who were paralyzed and men who were blind."

After Christmas Mrs. Earhart returned to Edwin in Kansas City, and Amelia went back to finish her senior term, but clearly neither Miss Sutherland nor the Ogontz School had anything further of value for Amelia Earhart. By February 1918, she had already received her mother's permission to leave without graduating and return to Toronto to nurse the war wounded.

From there, two letters to her mother survive.

> Toronto, [February 21, 1918]
>
> Mummy dear,
>
> The papers and letters were splendid and I enjoyed both. Awfully sorry to hear of your hard time running hither and yon and then on top to feel so miserable. I think we are having almost the same kind of horrid weather as you as sometimes it is frightfully hot for now and then will re-freeze and snow.
>
> Muriel is coming the weekend with me I think.
>
> Reg has asked me to so many things and I haven't gone once so finally consented to go to a senior professional hockey game on Saturday — not remembering at the time about Muriel. It is the game of season and he asked me a week in advance. Isn't that simple? I guess I'll cancel it.
>
> Mrs. [Mary] Holland has been lovely and taken me round so many places. I took her to hear Livitsky and he was wonderfully worth hearing. Mrs. Thomson has been dear and I have been often in to see her and she to see me. On Valentine's Day I bot eight little sweetheart roses, very small you know, smaller than the decoration on this paper, much — and pasted them by means of a red heart sticker (50 in a package for 10¢) on the doors of Mrs. Thomson, Mrs. Sylvester,

Mrs. Cameron and Mrs. Holland [residents at the St. Regis Hotel]. I think they were all very pleased. Also I sent Mr. Holland a Valentine about "pies," he is very fond of said article of diet and I saw it in a shop and sent it to him. He sent me one — fat cupids — too funny for words.

Your dear Valentine was the nicest thing I could ever have imagined. I thot it was my dear Mammy tho its writing was not yours.

My trunk is not here and I have written about it.

I am taking a V.A.D. course [Voluntary Aid Detachment]. I am using the library card and everyone has most kindly lent me books enough for a small library of my own...I am expecting the visit of an American girl tonight. She is a Southerner and is a designer of women's clothes etc. Rather nice. Her brother is a graduate of Cornell and now in Coast guard service. Picture very nice.

I have not heard from Ken or Harry or anybody for some days. I wish you would tell Pidge not to give up butter for Lent. It is simple. Muriel and I sent Miss Macdonald a box of violets and she was very pleased, Muriel said. She said it was just like you which is the greatest compliment she can give — and we can receive...

Oh, and I *did* hear from Ken. The enclosed clipping was published in one of the trade journals and he sent it — the magazine — to me. I think it is really splendid.

Zever (as Harry says)
Amelia

Toronto, [Spring, 1918]

Mummy dearest,

Enclosed are two letters. I sent you one from Peachie [Amelia's favorite aunt, widow of Amy's youngest brother Carl, now Mrs. A. L. Delaney] last evening, and a picture of her baby some time before...Hope you have received and will receive all O.K.

I *am* a busy person. I entered into a class of home nursing, etc. and am going on with the class altho they are half thru. The first day I showed everyone how to bandage tho, of course, didn't know myself. Mrs. Holland's physician asked me to come to his clinic — where he diagnoses and prescribes to poor people and asks the class to diagnose before he tells what really is the matter. That is not compulsory of course but I am getting everything I can. Also all lectures possible. I am going to see an operation if I can wheadle anybody into letting me.

I went to hockey game last night and was awfully thrilled — the skating is superb. I am going down (or up) for the girl this afternoon — she thot she would give up Sunday with me for Lent — not — I mean to indicate, because of the exquisite pleasure of seeing me, but to be able to go to church twice a week. Lent isn't supposed to aggravate the flesh alone and I shall pull her down by the ear. Bought two little cakes to be added inducement...

I am enclosing a letter from Muriel which she wrote me, as you see, at Miss Macdonald's instruction. It was necessary to be polite and write an acceptance so the enclosed was the result. Fancy Miss Macdonald's consternation if she'd seen it.

Affectionately

Amelia

L.O.L. for Paps as always.

These two letters, written before Easter 1918, were too early to give a picture of how hard Amelia worked during her few months as a nurse's aide at Spadina Military Hospital. Her duties included patient care from seven in the morning to seven at night with two hours off in the afternoon, and sometimes menial tasks such as scrubbing floors or washing up trays. Interested in diet, she attempted to improve hospital fare for the men; and to amuse them, she may have overcome her reluctance to play the piano for anyone but her father. Given her normal habit of whole-hearted involvement in whatever she undertook, her service was genuinely valuable.

Her life in Toronto was not all work. She was in good health, playing tennis and riding a rented horse from a nearby stable with her sister and friends she made among the hospital patients, who were British and French pilots. One of these, a captain in the Royal Flying Corps, stunted one afternoon for Amelia and Muriel. "At that moment," she wrote in *Last Flight*, "his little red airplane said something to me as it swished by." From then on, most of her free hours were spent at the airfield watching the RFC in training maneuvers.

The ultimate impact of her short nursing experience, however, was her intense pacifism. She believed the Crusades would have failed if women had journeyed with their knights into battle against the Saracens. In an article she wrote for *The Home Magazine* of August 1935, she proposed drafting women for war so they might share the "privilege of killing, suffering, maiming, wasting, paralyzing, impoverishing, losing mental and physical vigor, in shoveling under the dead and themselves dying gloriously." One can believe, however, that out of patriotism in World War II she would have joined Jacqueline Cochran and a number of other women pilots in ferrying warplanes around the United States and to Europe.

Amelia remained in Toronto until Armistice Day, when all the whistles blew and traffic was tied up and "Young men ran around with huge dusters of flour and blew it on young women," as she recalled in *The Fun of It*. But ". . .I didn't hear a serious word of thanksgiving in all the hullabaloo."

SIX

First Romance
1918-1920

The Armistice of November 11, 1918, not only constituted another watershed for Amelia Earhart, it preceded one of the first of several episodes of ill health coincident with periods of great stress in her life. She was through with boarding school, restless, undecided about a career, and she was seriously ill with a severe infection. One of the volunteers permitted night duty on the pneumonia ward, she apparently had kept well during the strenuous schedules required to cope with the great influenza epidemic which followed World War I and killed twenty million people around the world. Once the emergency was over, she took to her bed.

Today the illness would be diagnosed as sinusitis and dealt with handily, but in 1918 there were no antibiotics, and only irrigation of the sinus cavities was offered in the way of treatment. While the legend emphasized how she struggled to introduce tomatoes to the hospital diet and to substitute blancmange for rice pudding, nothing at all was ever mentioned about the effects of stress on her previously sheltered sensibilities. Witnessing aggravated suffering, open and suppurating wounds and bleeding stumps, while she scrubbed floors and washed patient trays and bedpans, in addition to performing other duties associated with bedside nursing, inevitably had an effect on her. As she recalled in the 1935 article for *The Home Magazine,* "There were incidents to remember. The first day I arrived someone pulled the fire alarm. Perhaps it was an accident, perhaps it was a fiendish joke. The result almost killed some of the [shellshocked] patients. They screamed and cried and rolled out of bed and we put them back and they rolled out again, begging us to give them something that would end their suffering."

Her body responded to sights and sounds and smells of distress in others with pain and pressure around one eye and copious drainage via the nostrils and throat. Despite the "washings out" as Amelia named the irrigations, the torment of chronic sinus infection persisted throughout the rest of her life, including illnesses or surgical attention following her marriage, and the flights of 1932 and 1935. Often there must have been periods of misery when she failed to mention her discomfort in writing to Amy. Amelia had learned early that one never complained of or ever admitted anything adverse or disagreeable about oneself or a family member.

She spent the spring of 1919 with her mother and sister in Northampton, Massachusetts, not well enough to attend college full time, but too well simply to sit around doing nothing. She signed up for a class in automobile engine repair at Smith College, where Muriel was now enrolled, and gained a skill which would later be useful in working with motor-driven vehicles, either on the ground or in the air.

With Amy and Muriel, Amelia spent that summer at Lake George, enjoying an outdoor regimen of swimming and canoeing, which improved her health even though she continued to have frequent headaches. Edwin, drawn into Christian Science, had overcome his drinking completely and, convinced there were better opportunities in Los Angeles, had left Kansas City. Now he wanted Amy to join him in California and resume their marriage. But Mrs. Earhart was not ready to go West. In the fall of 1919 when Amelia, now twenty-two, was to enter Columbia University as a premedical student, she accompanied her daughter to New York, ready as usual to inspect the premises and interview the head.

The following letter is undated, but it probably reflects the relationship between the two at the time. It also contains a definitive statement of Amelia's attitude toward religion.

New York, [?]

Dearest Mammy,

I was terribly disappointed not to see you off but I did not get out of class until *two ten* and sat and stared into a microscope until after four. It promises to be very interesting and I progressed very well because I was used to a microscope and fine work.

I reached the hotel a little after five and was presented with a bill for $1.10 that had come from our morning's breakfast. The which I paid from your generous deposit. The boy carried my suitcase and blanket all the way to Broadway and put me and them on a car...

Don't worry about meals or mentality. I didn't realize how the pipings of doubt had impressed you until you mentioned your worries today. Don't think for an instant I would ever become an atheist or even a doubter nor lose faith in the [Episcopalian] church's teachings as a whole. That is impossible. But you must admit there is a great deal radically wrong in methods and teachings and results to-day. Probably no more than yesterday, but the present stands up and waves its paws at *me* and I see — can't help it. It is not the clergy nor the church itself nor the people that are narrow, but the outside pressure that squeezes them into a routine. I can't say what I want briefly, and it is too late (for here) to say it lengthily. Lights are dimmed at 10 I believe...

Ever affectionately,

Amelia

I am generally cross and cranky but I love you the more after I come out of that mood. Final injunction

DON'T WORRY

A winter at Columbia convinced Amelia she was not destined to be a doctor, although her medical studies absorbed her. One of her professors later told how she mentally worked through an experiment while he was still lecturing on how to set it up. Medicine *per se* appealed to her; practicing it did not. When she fantasized herself at a sickbed dispensing placebos and moral support to a hypochondriac, honesty forced her to question her own sincerity. She found it inadequate. Rather than become a doctor, she decided to continue in medical research.

The family situation, however, was more on her mind than her future in April of 1920. Mrs. Earhart was to have minor surgery in Boston; she was still keeping an eye on Muriel at Northampton in the western part of the state, and Mr. Earhart was persisting in his efforts to bring the family to California. When Amelia wrote the following letter, it marked a change in relationship, not only between daughter and mother but also between the sisters, and in time it would affect Edwin himself.

> New York, [April 24, 1920]
>
> Dearest Angel Mammy,
>
> Where are you going to stay after the ether? *I think you should go immediately to Dickenson Hospital where you can have care and food* [italics added]. Have the D.o.D. (G. Stevens) present as she has some sense and is more careful than others. I suppose it is best to finish it up as the drain is so detrimental.
>
> I believe it will be best to all go together out west under the circumstances and have everything finished here in the east. The only alternative is to go together and have it done there, which has the *disadvantage* of delay and the *advantage* of our both being free and with you. However, do whichever you think best. I am glad of your trip to Boston.
>
> Don't worry over me, I am getting along splendidly...
>
> Lovingly,
> Amelia

She *believed*, she *thought*, what was best for Amy and for Muriel. Only late in the letter did she add "do whichever you think best," knowing almost instinctively that as she decreed so it would come to pass.

This unqualified self-assurance had developed from influences preceding her schooldays at Ogontz and more recently in Toronto, where she had a certain minor authority as a nurse's aide. Over and over again, she saw the doctors and nursing sisters give orders and make horrendous decisions for the patient's own good whether or not he was capable or willing to make his own. If this reasoning is correct, it is most unlikely Amelia was aware of the pattern, for she was rarely self-analytical. Nevertheless, she had earlier tried to assume the duties of head of family, unaware that doing so was to admit her father's failure as a husband and father. Now as Edwin would have done had he been there, and as she had seen it done in Toronto, Amelia was led to think and act for the good of those who might not think and act correctly for themselves. If this made her seem arrogant and patronizing to others, either she did not realize it or did not care.

As was natural, Mrs. Earhart, who was early conditioned to defer to her father and then to her husband, was more than willing to put her daughter in their place. She in particular, and Muriel on occasion, would look to Amelia for advice, and only rarely would they proceed without it. On one occasion Amelia reacted to their independence with a mild air of reproach. "I think it would have been better to let me know than to let things get so bad. . .I should prefer to pay the bills direct if you will have them forwarded here. . ." she would write in 1932 when an illness of her mother's had been kept from her. As usual, in the end, most decisions came down to money. Or the lack of it.

Amelia was always generous, she never failed her immediate family or other relatives, including her father, who needed help. As Amy later recalled, two precepts were hammered home in Amelia's youth: personal responsibility and everything given you is given you to share with others.

While Muriel remained at Smith College in the East, Amy went on ahead. Later Amelia took the train to California and joined her parents in the house Edwin found for them on Fourth Street in Los Angeles. She was bent on finishing her education in medical research, and in preventing another parental separation. At least until Muriel finished college. Then she promised herself to return to New York and her own life as she wanted to live it.

Long before the college year opened, she reverted to her Toronto habit by hanging around the several airfields in the Los Angeles area. She had never forgotten the little red airplane and what it said to her as it swished by. At the Long Beach airshow, Amelia persuaded her father to inquire how much it cost to learn to fly. One thousand dollars. An impossible sum. Soon after, she paid a dollar for ten minutes aloft in a plane piloted by Frank Hawks, who would later break many speed records in the air. From a field off Wilshire Boulevard the plane lifted over the friendly Hollywood hills, and at two or three hundred feet up Amelia knew she had to fly.

Nothing had prepared her for the physical and emotional impact of flight. No other urge, no intellectual, sexual, or social excitement ever involved or moved her as totally as soaring into the subtle environment where her most secret self was free of earthly concerns and subject to no human influence but her own. Here was the ultimate happiness, the physical and sensual as well as intellectual thrill for which no partner was needed, and no words were adequate.

All she lacked now was a thousand dollars.

She went to work at the telephone company in Los Angeles, and spent her weekends at a primitive airport on Long Beach Boulevard. This entailed an hour's ride on the streetcar and a walk of several miles from the end of the line. Once arrived at the windy, dusty hangar with its air sock, she blended into the scene. She had cut her hair, and with her slender figure in breeches and leather coat she mingled unobtrusively with the male pilots and mechanics.

She signed up on credit for flying lessons with Neta Snook, the first woman to graduate from the Curtiss School of Aviation, and she wrote to Muriel in Northampton that Snooky dressed and talked like a man and could do anything around a plane that a man could do. Snooky lectured Amelia on the ground, showed her the duplicate controls, and named the various parts of the Curtiss Canuck biplane used for training. Finally, seated in the rear cockpit Snooky taught Amelia her elementary maneuvers in the air. Whenever she wasn't practicing, Amelia was always somewhere around the pilots, ignoring profanity and asking questions with singleminded concentration. The word went around that Amelia Earhart was a "natural."

One can surmise that going to the airfield was not only a matter of need but a means of escape. Tension in the house on Fourth Street was gradually eroding the reconciliation between Amy and Edwin. Alcohol was not the problem; Edwin's situation was fairly prosperous and eminently respectable. Yet the financial pressure persisted, and to help out, the Earharts took in three young men as boarders.

One of them, Sam Chapman, was a New Englander, a chemical engineering graduate of Tufts University. He was Amelia's first serious suitor, and he always remained her close friend. The two enjoyed tennis and swimming, books and plays, and even attended a meeting of the proscribed International Workers of the World which was broken up by four policemen. Marriage and a conventional future for Amelia and Sam seemed certain to the family. But romance would always be secondary to Amelia. She was a realist and too sensitive not to have deep feelings about her parents' marital problems, and reservations on her own account. When it came to a choice, it seems clear that for Amelia, making love would always give way to flying. Furthermore, her independent nature bucked at the idea of joining other women who had little if any say in the disposition of their own lives. She liked Sam, she loved him, but she was already dedicated to aviation, and he wanted a wife who would stay at home and not seek a career of her own.

In later years, there would be a minimal amount of gossip, and the worst that was ever said of Amelia was that she was sexually promiscuous. Some people said she was having an affair with Fred Noonan, her navigator on the flight from which neither returned, the fact of his marriage to another woman shortly before takeoff being discounted. Other people would recall a supposed affair with Eugene Vidal, one of the founders of Transcontinental Air Transport, with whom Amelia was to work for many years. When the wife of Amelia's technical adviser, Paul Mantz, the noted stunt flyer, sued her husband for divorce, she would name Amelia as corespondent with Theresa Minor, who became his second wife. As Amelia herself would write to Amy of Mrs. Mantz, ". . . after her self inflicted publicity she will be watched. I really have been fortunate, for any one who has a name in the paper is a target for all sorts of things."

None of the gossip would really touch Amelia, even if she heard it, and for now, it was the weekend and time to put on her flying togs and go out to practice at the airfield. She was in search of a destiny which approached her as inexorably as she hurried forward to meet it.

SEVEN

Learning to Fly 1920-1928

When Muriel came out to visit in June, Amelia left her sister and Snooky on the ground to watch while she took off alone in a Kinner biplane. She went up to 5000 feet, where she "played around a little and came back," making a poor landing. Nothing special about the flight to her. Just her first solo! "It's so breath-takingly beautiful up there," she said, "I want to fly whenever I can." From then on, she saved every penny she could manage toward buying a plane of her own.

Advanced instruction under John Montijo, a former Army pilot, followed the solo, and during the week Amelia now worked in a photography studio to pay for the lessons. She carried a small camera with her wherever she went, photographing everything from garbage cans to an oil gusher as it came in and including experimental photographs of herself.

In September when Muriel's college bills were paid for her junior year at Smith, the family went into shock. Over the past four years, Mrs. Earhart's fortune had dwindled to $20,000. Obviously some means of preserving the capital had to be found. Sam Chapman had introduced the Earharts to a young civil engineer who with his partner was in need of money to work a promising gypsum mine. After lengthy and prudent investigation of the young men and the mine, located near the Moapa River Indian Reservation in Nevada, the family concurred in Mrs. Earhart's decision to sign an agreement and invest the last of her money.

On New Year's day of 1922 everything seemed to augur well for the Earhart family, and on the last weekend of January, Amelia and her father went to Nevada to visit the "Wedunit Mine." Peter Barnes and his partner Bill Chambers were anxious to have them see the work they had done and to talk happily of finishing the month's quota with two more truckloads of high-grade gypsum, which would keep their contract in force.

Because the Indian workers had moved to higher ground for fear of rain, Amelia and Edwin volunteered to shovel gypsum alongside the government Indian agent and his wife while Peter Barnes got one truckload across the Moapa River to a freight car on the siding and returned. As they worked to fill the second truck, clouds blew up out of the west and the rain begain. Hurriedly they assembled the mine records and surveying instruments, and both trucks left for headquarters in what was now a cloudburst.

Bill got his passengers across the weakened bridge, and they climbed out into ankle-deep water. Peter, in the second truck, hit the guardrail and pitched off as the bridge listed under its weight. When Bill clambered along a rope to the cab, he found Peter already dead of injuries from the crash.

Numbly Amelia and her father took Peter's body back to Las Vegas, and after the funeral delivered his suitcase, surveyor's tripod, and telescope to his parents. Since the men had agreed not to take salaries until the mine showed a profit, Amelia decided that the proceeds from the last gypsum sale should go to Peter's family and the remaining assets should go to Bill. Mrs. Earhart agreed, and Amelia wrote her sister, "There is no way that I can soften the blow for you. . . All of Mother's investment is gone. . ."

The next months were lightened only by the sale of the old Otis house on Quality Hill in Atchison, which unexpectedly gave Mrs. Earhart several hundred dollars. Muriel was finishing her junior year at Smith, and Amelia continued doggedly to work and fly, fly and work, as she saved her money for a plane. In the summer, she qualified for the only type of pilot's license issued at the time, the Fédération Aéronautique Internationale. She was now one of possibly a dozen licensed women flyers in the world.

Although Edwin thought flying unsafe and refused to leave the ground, Amy was supportive from the beginning, and in the end partly paid for Amelia's first plane. If she worried, she didn't show it, even when her daughter walked away from two minor crashes, neither due to pilot incompetence. Mrs. Earhart said later she was not apprehensive because Amelia ". . . had talked it over with the family, and I knew enough about her and of her general disposition to know that she would have to try it out, and if she did things, she always did them very carefully. She thought it out and her mind was quick and I had no special anxiety. . ."

No one believed in 1922, not even Amelia, that flying would prove to be more than just "having fun." Nevertheless, she was stubbornly determined to possess her own plane. For her twenty-fifth birthday on July 24, with all of her savings and all of Muriel's, plus additional funds from her mother, she bought a secondhand bright yellow Kinner Canary with a 3-cylinder air-cooled 60-horsepower engine. Later she wrote in *Last Flight* that the "motor was so rough my feet went to sleep after. . . a few minutes on the rudder bar." Nothing as unimportant as that, however, could dampen her pride and pleasure in owning her own plane.

In October at an air meet held at Rogers Field, with her sister and father watching from the bleachers, Amelia took off and rapidly climbed out of sight. She stayed up for almost an hour, and when she finally landed, officials surrounded her plane to retrieve a sealed barograph installed under the sponsorship of the California Aero Club. Almost at once loudspeakers announced that Amelia Earhart had broken the altitude record for women by flying to 14,000 feet. Amelia was already on her way to confer with the mechanics and find out why her engine had failed before she could go higher. A spark control lever had become disconnected, they told her, adding their congratulations.

The record stood for only a few weeks, but it was her first "first."

After Ruth Nichols broke it, Amelia made an effort to better the new record. Flying blind in snow that stung her face and blanked her goggles, she had to spin out at 12,000 feet, coming down by gravity and not breaking cloud until she reached 3000 feet. Frightened but not admitting it, she landed and with a cool smile turned aside uncomplimentary remarks on her descent. Concerning danger she believed that Hamlet would have made a bad flyer because "he worried too much."

Since the completion of their education was impossible for the sisters, Muriel taught fourth grade in a Los Angeles school for the next two years and Amelia continued to work at various jobs and to fly as often as she could. Their parents were increasingly unhappy, and in 1924 Amy and Edwin Earhart reached the end of their twenty-nine-year marriage. He was granted an uncontested divorce, and the three Earhart women decided to make their home together on the East Coast.

Muriel went on ahead to work toward a degree in Education at Harvard during the summer, and Sam Chapman said he intended to follow Amelia to Boston. The fearful notion of flying Mrs. Earhart East was put down by all members of the family, and Amelia was persuaded instead to sell the Kinner Canary. She bought a Kissel touring car, also bright yellow, with a collapsible top, wire wheels, spare tires ahead of the passenger doors, and two steps on each side for running boards.

In the late spring Amelia put Amy in the "Yellow Peril" and left for Boston on a rambling itinerary that went north via Yosemite and Crater Lake, turned east from Seattle to Banff and Lake Louise, headed south for Yellowstone, and finally picked up the airmail beacons stationed along the Lincoln Highway near Cheyenne, which thrilled Amelia. After the long transcontinental drive over two-lane roads too primitive to be called highways, which included visits with relatives and friends along the way, Amelia and Amy took a house with Muriel in Medford, five miles north of Boston. A former shipbuilding center, it was a suitably quiet and respectable old town for the three Earhart women, and it later became Muriel's permanent place of residence.

Within a week of their arrival, Amelia entered Massachusetts General Hospital in Boston for surgery. During the four stressful years in California, while Edwin and Amy struggled to preserve their marriage, and Amelia acted as a buffer between them, she had never been free of headache and nasal discomfort. Her flying had not helped the condition. The goggles and helmet she wore did not entirely protect her face from the effect of wind and cold in an open cockpit, and she had constantly endured probes and irrigations which never brought more than temporary relief. During her hospital stay, a small piece of bone was surgically removed to allow natural drainage from the offending antrum. For the first time in years, she was free of headache and nasal discomfort, but the difficulty would return and she would mention other attacks after periods of great stress in the future.

Restless after her recovery, Amelia went to New York for the winter semester in pre-med at Columbia, and dropped out for the summer, returning to Boston. Since Muriel was teaching, she decided to teach also. Instructing foreign students in English proved only an annoyance. Classes were held in the late afternoon or evening anywhere within thirty miles of Boston, the pay was meager, and there was no allowance for transportation.

In 1925 Amelia went to Harvard summer school, and after that to do social work at Denison House in Boston, teaching English part time to the Syrians and Chinese in the neighborhood. Marion Perkins, the head worker, was perceptive enough to give Amelia free rein in her desire to "give boys and girls the experience that will keep them young," as she put it about her day students. She loved the work and delighted in contacting cultures and ways of life different from her own. In the following year, she was made a full-time resident worker at sixty dollars a month, and given an apartment on the top floor of Denison House. Frequently she took some of the girls home to Medford for picnics in the yard or storytelling by the fireplace, and often in the Yellow Peril she gave the smaller children their very first ride in an automobile.

Sam Chapman had indeed followed Amelia to Boston, and when she wasn't working, they went with Muriel and her friend Albert Morrissey, a Navy veteran whom she later married, to Marblehead for swimming, clamming, and cookouts on the Neck. Louise de Schweintz, a friend from Columbia who was doing her internship at Boston Hospital, joined them occasionally with her fiancé. Medicine still fascinated Amelia, and Louise once permitted her to watch a woman give birth, but a medical career was out. She didn't know exactly what she would do with the rest of her life; it was easier to discover what she wouldn't do.

Sam was intent on marriage but he disliked the idea of working wives, and Amelia had no intention of subsiding into domesticity. He believed she objected to his irregular hours with the Boston Edison Company; this only annoyed her. "He should do whatever makes him happiest," she told Muriel. As for herself, "I know what I want to do and I expect to do it, married or single." The romance was over, but the friendship endured. In 1937 a member of Sam's family wrote to Mrs. Earhart that he didn't like to talk about Amelia's disappearance, that he was very upset and seemed without hope that she would be found. In the years between, however, they remained in touch and often saw each other when she was on the East Coast.

Because she was so good at it, and seemed happy enough, Amy and Muriel believed Amelia had found a natural vocation in social work, not realizing that Amelia's reluctance to display her innermost feelings made her sometimes appear what she was not. Her heart was still in the sky. She joined the Boston Chapter of the National Aeronautic Association and ultimately became its vice president. Any free hours on weekends, she gravitated to the nearest airfield.

When W. G. Kinner wrote asking her to find a sales agent for the Canary, she happened to meet Harold T. Dennison in the course of her search, and ended by scratching together a sum of money to invest in the Dennison Airport near Squantum. Not finding the agent Kinner had wanted, moreover, she took on the job herself and was able to demonstrate the Canary for prospective buyers, and occasionally to use it for her own enjoyment.

Never thinking of it as a life work, Amy encouraged Amelia's flying as she had in Los Angeles. She wrote later, "I realized that if she wanted to be a flyer someone in the family had to be interested and had to go with her and help her out...Her relatives thought her flying was decidedly queer. Some — the younger ones — thought it might be interesting and weren't so thoroughly against it as those of the relatives who were older — they felt it was not only a dangerous thing for her, but it was a very impracticable way of getting over the earth."

In 1927 when Charles A. Lindbergh made the first transatlantic flight, the idea of the same flight for herself lodged in Amelia's subconscious. Perhaps even in her conscious. Certainly she never hesitated in April of 1928 when Captain Hilton H. Railey, acting for a friend in New York, telephoned Denison House to ask if she would be interested in doing something hazardous for aviation. Shortly after the call, Amelia went to New York for an interview with publisher George Palmer Putnam, attorney David T. Layman, and John Phipps, a brother of wealthy Mrs. Frederick Guest. Born in America and English by marriage, Amy Guest was a pioneer pilot herself. Wanting to be the first woman to fly the Atlantic, she bought Commander Richard E. Byrd's trimotored Fokker and made preparations for the trip. Her family refused to let her, but as a friendly gesture to the two countries she loved, she insisted the flight must continue. In the plane she demanded the presence of an American woman pilot from a family of distinction.

Who else but Amelia Earhart? Her antecedents reached back to England, and without knowing it she had been preparing for such an opportunity ever since a small red plane had whisked across her vision in Toronto ten years earlier. She could no more refuse than she could stop breathing. At the conclusion of the interview, she had committed herself. Destiny and Amelia Earhart had come face to face, and although she never gave a thought to becoming an instant celebrity, publisher and promoter George Palmer Putnam was already at work devising ways and means of creating and exploiting a flying heroine to match Lindbergh.

EIGHT

"A Sack of Potatoes" 1928

Amelia's personal preparations for the transatlantic flight were simple. At Denison House, she told Marion Perkins about her plans and was promised a two weeks' leave of absence to protect her job. She confided in Sam Chapman, telling him her will was in a safety deposit box at a West Medford bank. In it she listed dental and hospital expenses of a thousand dollars, and assets including the Yellow Peril, a United States Treasury Bond, and stock in the Kinner Airplane Company and the Dennison Airport at Squantum. After the debts were paid, she directed that any remainder go to Mrs. Earhart, an intention she repeated when she signed her final will and testament on April 5, 1932.

Also to Sam, Amelia entrusted a letter to her sister to be opened when the *Friendship* took off from Boston. To Muriel, she said she had tried to play for a large stake, "and if I succeed all will be well. If I don't, I shall be happy to pop off in the midst of such an adventure. My only regret is leaving you and mother stranded for a while... Sam will tell you the whole story. Please explain all to mother. I couldn't stand the added strain of telling mother and you..."

Not even flying the Atlantic could lift Amelia's sense of responsibility for her mother and sister. Years earlier when Amy and Edwin were straining apart, she had possibly considered not returning to Ogontz. She termed herself "a selfish and guilty daughter," in a letter to her mother in 1917, "I have awful twinges of conscience about leaving you..."

The words were as applicable now as they had been eleven years before. Amy Earhart was alone, and she must have been lonely. In California Edwin had remarried, and in Medford Muriel was teaching and newly engaged to Albert Morrissey. Amelia spent her time either at Denison House or Dennison Airport. Beyond shopping and attending church, where she made acquaintances at once, Amy kept house for herself and Muriel and maintained a voluminous correspondence among family and old friends. She was totally dependent on a hearing aid now and she wrote later that sometimes she was so "tired and nervous" she couldn't sleep. In the ordinary course of affairs, she had "lost" both daughters, a circumstance she did not acknowledge even if she realized it until she later commented, "at the beginning of that part of her life [Amelia] talked over things with me just as she always had. Of course, later on when she had no time even to talk to herself, I had to feel then she was getting away from me..."

The transatlantic flight was kept secret, however, and because no one, least of all Amelia, minimized the hazards of the attempt, it could happen that Amy was about to lose her older daughter in the cruelest sense. Some daughters might have considered their responsibility stronger than their own needs, and sacrificed the opportunity. Not Amelia. Driven by her own nature, her need to fly, to compete with men, to achieve what no woman had ever attempted before, Amelia saw no choice. Flying lured her as no man ever would, and responsibility would later be discharged with gifts and money.

Amelia gave separate letters, unopened until 1937, to George Putnam to hold for her parents. To her mother, she wrote, "Even tho I have lost the adventure it was worth while. Our family tends to be too secure. My life has really been very happy and I didn't mind contemplating its end in the midst of it." Always freer with her father, she wrote, "Hooray for the last grand adventure! I wish I had won but it was worth while anyway. You know that.

I have no faith that we'll meet anywhere again, but I wish we might..." She loved her parents, she hoped not to cause them grief, but whatever the cost, she was completely unable to resist a unique and ideal opportunity that was unlikely ever to be repeated.

Such tight security surrounded preparations for the flight that Amelia, although technically captain of the plane, was forbidden to go to the Boston Airport where the *Friendship* was being made ready. She met often with the two men who would be her flight crew, pilot Wilmer L. (Bill) Stultz and mechanic Louis (Slim) Gordon, at the Boston home of Commander Richard E. Byrd who was technical consultant for the project. The latter with Floyd Bennett had been first to fly over the North Pole, and in the following year, with Bernt Balchen as radio operator and photographer, Byrd would be first to fly over the South Pole. Former Army Captain Hilton H. Railey, an adventurous newspaperman from the South, acted as public relations officer and George Palmer Putnam represented the sponsors.

Amelia saw the Fokker only once during the long weeks of preparation. Originally a land plane fitted with wheels, attaching pontoons in case of a water landing made it the first trimotored seaplane. Each of its three Wright Whirlwind engines was capable of 225 horsepower, and from wingtip to wingtip it measured approximately 72 feet. It was painted bright orange in case an accident required a rescue search, and its cabin was crowded with two large gas tanks and a table for navigational instruments. There were no passenger seats.

Twice delayed by fog, the *Friendship* finally flew off on the first leg of the flight on the morning of June 3, 1928, with Amelia crouching behind the pilot. Even before the plane was out of sight, George Putnam called a news conference and with Captain Railey informed the world that a woman flyer had just taken off by air for Halifax en route to England. That same day the *Christian Science Monitor* ran one of the first publicity stories about Amelia Earhart under the headline: BOSTON WOMAN FLIES INTO DAWN ON SURPRISE TRANSATLANTIC TRIP.

Typical of many articles and stories that would follow, it mixed up dates and times of Amelia's history, saying among other inaccuracies that she had taken degrees at Columbia and the University of Southern California, and had done graduate work at Harvard. It noted that "A light fog laid pearl dust on the face of the water," as the plane rose, and the caption above a head and shoulders photo read, "She Has the Lindbergh Look."

Slim and short-haired, she did look like the Colonel; in flying togs the resemblance was more marked. She too was shy, modest, and dedicated to advancing the cause of aviation. In time she apologized by letter to Mrs. Lindbergh for what she termed the "ridiculous publicity" that dubbed her "Lady Lindy." Not because she didn't appreciate the comparison but because it was "quite unjustified." She would have disowned the nickname, but the public loved it and it stuck.

The "look" also inspired George Palmer Putnam. He wanted a companion volume to Lindbergh's *We*, a coup which the Putnam firm had already published. When he heard that Commander Byrd had sold his plane to a wealthy woman who "plans to fly the Atlantic," he suggested to Captain Railey that they "crash the gate" and "cash in" on what he considered a stunt. He told Railey to locate the plane and "pump the pilots" for information.

Instinct served him well. Although she didn't know it, he was now and would be for the rest of Amelia's life the promoter and developer of the AE legend, never letting her coattails go, not even after her death. In 1928 he was thirty-nine years old, married to the former Dorothy Binney, and the father of two sons, aged nine and twelve. A tall lean man, full of impatient energy, his talent lay in propelling others to the celebrity status he never managed for himself, a source of personal displeasure that showed when he thrust himself into every conversation, every interview, every photograph he possibly could. Reporters complained later that to get a few words from Amelia they had to listen to hundreds from him.

On first meeting, Amelia had been impressed with GP, as he

wished to be called. "A fascinating man," she had told Marion Perkins upon her return from the New York interview. He had driven with her in a taxi, and "Once he got me to the station, he hustled me aboard the Boston train like a sack of potatoes. Didn't offer to pay my fare back home either!"

The *Friendship* made its way to Halifax for overnight, and on June 4 sat down amid a welcoming flotilla of small boats at Trepassey, Newfoundland. Despite Amelia's concern with weather conditions, the performance of the plane, the two men with her, and the hazardous nature of the adventure ahead, she took time to compose a wire for her mother: KNOW YOU WILL UNDERSTAND WHY I COULD NOT TELL PLANS OF FLIGHT STOP DONT WORRY STOP NO MATTER WHAT HAPPENS IT WILL HAVE BEEN WORTH THE TRYING STOP LOVE-A. Her mother wired back: WE ARE NOT WORRYING STOP WISH I WERE WITH YOU STOP GOOD LUCK AND CHEERIO STOP LOVE- MOTHER. A gallant lady's response to an overwhelming surprise.

Amy and Muriel were already a part of the legend. Sam Chapman had been delegated to tell them the news, but before he could get to the house a reporter telephoned. "What do you think of your daughter flying overseas?" he asked Mrs. Earhart, who snapped, "I think she is too smart to try it." Then she had to "eat" her words, of course. When the Boston papers came out in the afternoon, the publicity precipitated a storm of reporters around the Earhart house. They asked many personal questions which Amy and Muriel resented, and demanded any and all available photographs of Amelia, who had no more idea of the fame about to envelop her than her mother and sister had.

Amy said later, ". . .she never liked publicity. . .she was very conservative in some ways underneath. I think it puzzled her more. . ." The mask Amelia later developed to hide behind was always calm and always cool, and some people took it for its own sake, never understanding how warm and sensitive was the woman behind it. She was also vulnerable, and the demanding pressures of fame would force her to respond with always greater efforts to preserve and justify the legend simply because in the beginning it was hollow. And no one knew that better than she, nor made greater efforts to keep the record straight. Over and over, directly and by implication, she said the success of the *Friendship* flight was due to the skill of Stultz and Gordon, and had nothing to do with her presence aboard. "But I happened to be a woman," she wrote later in *The Fun of It*, "and the first to make a transatlantic crossing by air, and the press and the public seemed to be more interested in that fact than any other. Though palpably unfair, the circumstance was unavoidable."

Amelia had her first taste of "disgusting publicity" when the Boston papers arrived at Trepassey and she read how she hoped for enough money to "pay off the mortgage on the family home." In fact Stultz would receive $20,000 and Gordon $5000, but Amelia's only recompense was making the flight. And anyway the house was rented. As time passed and the *Friendship* waited at anchor on Trepassey Bay for favorable weather, a critical attack appeared in one Boston paper intimating that she was delaying the flight out of fear, a canard which George Putnam promptly and efficiently denied.

GP was in frequent telegraphic communication with Amelia, relaying weather reports from "Doc" James H. Kimball of the United States Weather Bureau in New York. At the same time, she and Slim Gordon were increasingly doubtful if Bill Stultz would be sober enough to fly when the weather turned. At one point Gordon threatened to walk out if Amelia didn't send for the backup pilot waiting on call in Boston. Uneasily she persuaded him to wait a bit longer, since as captain of the ship, responsibility for the decision was hers alone. She had to consider what was safe, what professional and emotional damage a replacement would do to Bill, and what the sponsors might think of her. Unhappily reminded of her father's problem, she pulled Bill away from the bottle to walk with her and Gordon on the beach, or she and Slim played endless games of rummy while Bill drank alone in his room.

On June 17, when Doc Kimball finally said the weather

promised fair over the North Atlantic for the next forty-eight hours, Stultz was hopelessly drunk. Amelia left the code word "Violet" to be telegraphed to Putnam a half hour after departure, and with Slim pulled and hauled Bill into the plane. Finding a bottle hidden in the cabin, Amelia dumped it.

Once at the controls, however, Stultz somehow straightened up and made three unsuccessful tries to take off across the uneven waters of the bay. On the fourth attempt, Amelia, stopwatch in hand, saw the air-speed indicator reach the required fifty miles an hour for takeoff — and pass it. The *Friendship*, with two motors coughing salt water, was aloft and committed.

For 20 hours and 40 minutes, Amelia crouched at the chart table staring out the window, with only short naps to break the tension. She kept the logbook faithfully, filling it with technical data concerning the weather and the performance of the plane, and interlining with her frequent personal observations: "I think I am happy — sad admission of scant intellectual equipment. I am getting housemaid's knee kneeling here at the table gulping beauty . . ."

Eventually Bill Stultz brought the *Friendship* down in a perfect landing at Burry Port, Wales, on the morning of June 18. To that moment, only twenty-seven men had succeeded in seven attempts to fly the Atlantic. Now the crossing had been made by two more. And the first woman.

Amelia had with her two scarves, a toothbrush, and a comb, and when the villagers after a two-hour delay finally gathered to greet the flyers, one of her scarves disappeared. Trivia of this nature were prominent on the panorama of GP's publicity, and even Amelia later remarked on how often people only wanted to know what she wore and what she had with her in the way of personal possessions.

Badly in need of food and rest, the flyers greeted Captain Railey, who, after waiting in England for two weeks, flew up from Southampton as soon as word of the landing reached him. The townfolk, managed by three bewildered constables, outdid themselves, and dinner was delayed until ten o'clock that night. Shortly after, Captain Railey agreed to send cables to Mrs. Earhart and Marion Perkins; LOVE — AMELIA was all she could think of to send. Then he shepherded the exhausted three to rooms in the Ashburnham Hotel.

On the following day, they bade their new friends goodbye and took off in the lightly refueled *Friendship* for Southampton where Mrs. Frederick Guest and the Lady Mayor, along with other dignitaries and citizens, were waiting to greet the flyers.

Once in the air over Wales, Amelia was finally allowed a turn at the controls, no longer "just a sack of potatoes" as she called herself on the trip. She conceded that without her, or a woman like her, Mrs. Guest would not have sponsored the flight, but she concealed any pride she might have taken in her own resolute courage, and attributed credit not only to her crew but to "the flight's backers as well as the manufacturers of the plane and the motors."

She was stunned by the official reception at Southampton, with tugboats whistling and steamer foghorns blasting a welcome, and overwhelmed by the cheering throngs on the city streets and along the road to London. Surely there the excitement would die down and she would be anonymous again, Amelia Mary Earhart, female, not quite thirty-one, American, licensed pilot, and exceedingly shy of publicity, along for the ride and truly unworthy of great attention.

Instant recognition and acclaim whenever she appeared in London quickly proved she could no longer be anonymous. Whether she wanted to be or not, whether she deserved to be or not, she was a famous personage. Her privacy, her inner self, was no longer safe from invasion or examination, and her disclaimers went unheard in the cheers and applause of strangers; all those eyes staring at her, those mouths yelling at her, those hands plucking her sleeve or reaching to pat her cheek or shoulder or backside, without ever feeling how she shrank from them, how she wanted to run and hide in the dark somewhere, alone but not lonely, only relieved to be safe again.

The only way to cope was to put on the mask her mother would later describe when she said, "[Amelia] really didn't feel safe anywhere, and she had to put on an outside." Amazing how rapidly the air of cool calm concealment became natural, how remote and protected Amelia felt behind it, and how in the end it prevented her coming to believe the legend, which was already born and burgeoning.

NINE

Proposal
of Marriage
1928-1929

After a fortnight's "jumble of teas, theatres, speech making, exhibition tennis, polo and Parliament," Amelia and her crew, along with Captain Railey, sailed for New York on the *President Roosevelt*, a restful interlude, but not quite. The ship's captain, Harry Manning, gave Amelia practical instruction in navigation which she had not had, Bill Stultz gave her a bad time with his drinking, and the other passengers never gave up trying to lionize her. In solitude, she reflected on events of the past two weeks.

She had talked to her mother by telephone and received a congratulatory cable from President Calvin Coolidge, to which she replied: SUCCESS ENTIRELY DUE GREAT SKILL OF MR. STULTZ STOP...She shopped at Selfridge's in London where she was not permitted to pay for her modest purchases, and she danced with the Prince of Wales, who would become Edward VIII and abdicate his throne. She squeezed in a visit to Toynbee Hall, upon which Denison House was patterned, and slipped away by herself early one morning to meet with Lady Mary Heath at Croyden Airdrome. She spent two hours flying the Avro Avian Moth in which England's foremost woman pilot had flown alone from Cape Town, South Africa, to London. Amelia liked the little plane so well she bought it and arranged to have it shipped home.

She still planned to return to Denison House and the "work I love," write the promised book for G. P. Putnam's Sons, and decide what her future would be. She was a month short of being thirty-one and age seemed important, since she genuinely had no idea that her public future was already decided. While still aboard the *President Roosevelt*, however, she received a radiogram from George Putnam. Thirty-two cities had invited the crew of the *Friendship* to civic receptions, and GP had decided they should go from New York to Boston, then to Medford in deference to her family, and on to Chicago during the first week of their return. As Amelia put it later, if she had accepted all the invitations offered, she "might not have got home in a year and a day."

The New York reception was a swirl of civic and national dignitaries who took her off the ship and up the harbor on the Mayor's barge. On the folded canvas top of a convertible roadster, she rode through a storm of confetti and torn telephone books to City Hall. There Mayor Jimmy Walker presented a medal and a key to the city which GP came out of the shadows to slip into his pocket for safekeeping.

Next day at the Boston Airport, Mrs. Earhart and Muriel were waiting when Amelia flew in for a cosier celebration. She stepped from the plane, ducked her head before the cameras, and went to kiss Amy. "How are you, Ma? Hello, Sis." Asked to remove her straw hat for the photographers, she threw it to Muriel. "Here's where I get sixty more freckles on my poor nose, I guess."

Along the parade route, children from Denison House called out their names to her, "Hi, Miss Earhart, it's me, Sammy — Arfreda — Marak" or any of a dozen others, and Amelia smiled and called back "Hi, there!" to each one. In the evening at a formal dinner, Commander Byrd called her a "gallant lady," and Amelia made the usual disclaimer by presenting Stultz and Gordon as "the men who made aviation history." When the celebration ended, GP was waiting at the curb to turn over the Yellow Peril, and Amelia thankfully took the keys and drove her mother and sister home to Medford for a family visit.

GP. George Palmer Putnam. Already he had taken over. After

Chicago, he said, Amelia would write her book in the seclusion of his home at Rye, New York, with a secretary to help. He said once the book was out, she would begin a lecture series for handsome fees. He said he would act as her unofficial manager and adviser on what commercials to endorse and what newspaper and magazine articles to write. And while the hullabaloo kept up, he said, she would be unable to go back to her social work. If Amelia had reservations, she didn't voice them, and probably under the onslaught of sudden fame she was grateful to him for guidance in handling the new and amazing demands being made upon her.

When the smaller reception was over in Medford, Sam Chapman took Amelia off for a few hours to Marblehead to relax. A day later, she and the two pilots were in Chicago, and by then Amelia was exhausted and glad to return to New York by train, leaving Stultz and Gordon on their own. Almost certainly she never saw either of them again.

The large comfortable Putnam house at Rye was off a main road, almost hidden by oaks and elms where dogwood bloomed prolifically in the spring. The living room was long and wide enough to accommodate an unfolded parachute, as Amelia would later demonstrate after she became Mrs. GP. Outside was a terrace from which a long flight of steps led down to a lily pond and a level area for croquet. Upstairs were spacious bedrooms and bathrooms almost as large. Amelia loved the place, not only for its beauty but for its privacy.

She worked faithfully on the story of the *Friendship* flight, to be titled *20 Hrs. 40 Min.*, and she liked Dorothy Binney Putnam so well, she dedicated the book to her host's wife.

Before the manuscript was completed, Amelia was immersed in discussions with promoters, airline operators, and educators; she considered offers to lecture before groups all over the country. And then there was the fan mail. At the rate of 200 letters a day. She read it all and answered most of it by "squiggling" her autograph on a postcard, or dictating to a stenographer. Occasionally she ran across a letter from an old friend or family acquaintance, "I could picture you... You were always ready for adventure..." Or from strangers, "You don't know me, but I thought of you all the way over to England, and added my prayers to those of many..."

In August she went to New York, where she stayed at the Hotel Seymour, 50 West 45th Street. From there she wrote an unsigned note to her mother:

> [New York, August 12, 1928]
> Staying here one night. Byrd's dinner, Theater, Jimmy Walkers. Hooray.
> Enclosed letter from Mary Holland [her Toronto friend]. Thot you'd like to see. Sent package to P[idge]. Hope she can use things. If you know something she wants get it for her and I'll pay. Also you. My treat, at last.
> Just opened your letter... can't understand. I am protected here. No one gets to me. If the Hearst reporter annoys you, wire me and I can have it stopped. Don't worry, but be careful about telling people whereabout I am.

Inevitably the close relation between Amy and Amelia was in transition. Mrs. Earhart, gaunt but vigorous at almost sixty, and genuinely unworldly, was properly reticent and disdainful of publicity for *nice* people except in discreet notices of birth, marriage, and death. Amelia, on the other hand, had quickly learned how to handle reporters, how to get things done on demand, and how to mingle comfortably with the famous. From now on she saw her mother as often as she possibly could, frequently asked her along on lecture circuits, and in every way tried to share her own new life. That she failed was the fault of neither.

Nor were changing relations with Muriel anyone's fault. If there had been sibling rivalry, each had cause at the moment to enjoy a triumph over the other. Amelia was now famous and set on her career in aviation and Muriel was preparing for her wedding. But as Muriel has repeatedly said, they were not rivals; each relished what she had without resentful envy of the other.

Probably neither completely understood the fundamental energies that drove them in different ways toward different goals. Amelia could see nothing but frustration for herself in marriage unless she could have her career too, and she feared Muriel would sink into marriage and motherhood and never have a career at all. Muriel saw nothing but total joy ahead even if she might be forced to give up her career, and she feared that if Amelia failed to marry Sam Chapman now, she would eventually lose him. In fact, neither fear came true. After Muriel's two children were old enough, she resumed her education and enjoyed a good career in teaching. Amelia and Sam remained constant and loyal friends to the end of her life.

Now it was only 1928, however, and completely opposite points of view posed no problem; but a question of Muriel's discretion concerning Amelia's affairs, whether justified or not, seemed important, as noted in the following letter:

Rye, August 26, 1928

Dear Mammy,

I got back to N.Y. with hardly a recognition. Muriel called shortly after I arrived asking whether I was to fly to Utica or not. I can't tell so far ahead and thot it dumb of [Merwin Hart, a pilot friend] to have her ask.

Perhaps you'd better not talk my intimate details of salary and business with Pidge. I don't want her to spread the news and always fear she will.

I think I have an apartment, but will let you know later.

To repeat: the stuff in the corner may be packed any way you see fit, for shipment here. Foil and tennis racquet also.

Photographic things, in the boxes under the couch

and bed could be stored at Denny or somewhere where they could be got at in case I wanted them.

If we decide not to send the overstuffers down here they will be put in Metropolitan Storage and the photographics with them. I don't know yet about the furnishings required.

I enjoyed my stay in Beantown and wish it could have been longer.

Please throw away rags and get things you need on my account at Filene's [Boston department store]. I'll instruct them. I can do it now and the pleasure is mine.

When and if the reporters come to you please refer them to Mr. Putnam. Don't even say yes or no if you don't want to. Just say you can add nothing to their tales and to ask me or GPP. Tell em you know many of my plans but are not divulging.

Your doter,
A.E.

In September *20 Hrs. 40 Min.* was finished, and the Avian Moth having arrived from England, Amelia purchased a "lovely assortment of air navigation maps" and took off in her new plane from a nearby polo field, alone and on holiday. Still with no definite plan for the future, she was joyful to "be a vagabond — in the air."

She flew to Los Angeles, taking a leisurely route, and while visiting her father and friends attended the National Air Races. Then she turned around and flew back to New York, achieving another record thereby, the first woman to make a solo round-trip transcontinental flight.

In New York George Putnam had her first lecture tour all arranged, and from now on, almost without exception, fall, winter and spring would be devoted to one-night stands on the circuit. Universities, colleges, men's clubs, women's clubs, civic forums, everyone wanted to hear Amelia Earhart speak. She was the most popular woman in America, the most famous in the world, her simplicity, coupled with her honesty and courage, making an indelible impression on those who applauded her.

McCall's Magazine offered her the position of staff editor for aviation until a cigarette was advertised as the brand the crew of the Friendship had carried, when the offer was withdrawn. Since Amelia did not smoke, she had at first refused to sign the endorsement, but the company then refused to pay Stultz and Gordon. So she complied, and donated her $1500 to Commander Byrd for his second Antarctic expedition. Although Putnam forced McCall's to renew its offer, Amelia was by then an associate editor of Cosmopolitan, committed to producing eight articles a year on aviation.

First and always, however, there were the lectures. A typical month might include engagements in twenty-seven Midwestern cities, the few remaining days allotted to moving from one city to another, and no time provided for rest. Sometimes there were two lectures in one day, and possibly an important social engagement squeezed in between. And always in the morning, or perhaps the night before, the move to the next city.

Whatever Amelia may have expected when she agreed to join the Friendship, she could not have anticipated such a grueling routine. This was the period in which her mother said she had "no time even to talk to herself." If Amy worried about the strain on Amelia, she was the first to acknowledge that while "It was at times more than a human being could bear, fortunately, she [was like] her father — when she reached a certain stage of exhaustion she was able to lie down and go right to sleep."

Amelia seemed to thrive on the schedules. In December she wrote to her mother from aboard the Norfolk and Washington steamer District of Columbia:

[December 17, 1928]

Dear Mammie,

This is a pleasant junket. We are sailing down the broad Potomac in a quivering little tub. All hands are carefree and it doesn't matter that we're two or three hours late.

There is a nice crowd aboard and everywhere one goes one hears terms aeronautical. I was considered important enough to be the guest of the Government so I'm riding free and eating free. We shall stop at Langley to see more wind tunnels and experimental stuff. The foreign delegates are very good scouts. I am bunking with Elizabeth Warner — Secy Warner's sister. Secy. Davison and wife are aboard. Senator Bingham and wife and several officials.

It's the kind of junket you'd like and had I had any idea I was going I should have arranged for your coming . . .

A.E.

Presumably Amelia spent the Christmas holidays with her mother and sister in Medford, but soon into 1929 she took up the lecture trail again, speaking here one night and somewhere else the next.

Aboard the "Sunshine Special"
March 7, 1929

Dear Mammy,

Today's your birthday. I'm sorry I had to be away. Anyway I bring a sprize when I return.

It seems funny to be riding on the M.P. [Missouri Pacific] without a pass. The same old bumps are in the road-bed. It has been very cold but after St. Louis it has begun to warm up a bit.

I have worked all day and am tired tonight. I have written several things I've been wanting to . . .

I'll be home on 13th if not before.

A.E.

In moments snatched on trains or in hotel rooms, Amelia wrote her articles for *Cosmopolitan*, choosing such themes as safety in flying, airport facilities, pilot training, letting a daughter fly, and feminine fears of flying. In addition to her own lecture schedule, she now traveled for Transcontinental Air Transport, an ancestor of Trans World Airlines, speaking before Chambers of Commerce and various businessmen's groups in an effort to stimulate passenger interest in scheduled flights.

Colonel Lindbergh was chairman of the TAT technical committee, and the pilot founders were Eugene Vidal, formerly of the Army Air Corps, and Paul Collins, a veteran airmail flyer. Analysis had shown TAT that if wives were reassured of aviation safety, more men would use a regular airline service in their business travel. Amelia went out to persuade the women.

Placed in charge of the traffic department, she helped maintain flight schedules and urged both ground and air crews to satisfy the curiosity of some passengers and allay the fears of others. For herself, she was able to use TAT planes to get around if she were disinclined to fly her own. At every opportunity she took Mrs. Earhart with her and frequently soothed worried mothers with a description of how fearless Amy was.

Late in June, Muriel married Albert Morrissey, and although Amelia was fogbound in New Jersey and missed the rehearsal and party on the wedding eve, she was present next day as her sister's maid of honor. After the ceremony, when she was complimented for the *Friendship* flight she answered, "I think what Pidge has just done took more courage than my flying did." She considered the Lindberghs to be happily married, but remembered too clearly the unhappiness of her parents. Unless she found a man who would share responsibility equally and leave her free to pursue flying, she doubted she would ever marry.

In August she and Amy were in Los Angeles for overnight at the Westlake Hotel before Amy took the train back to New York, leaving Amelia to see that her new Lockheed Vega, bought with proceeds from the sale of the Avian Moth, was ready for the first Women's Air Derby. On August 16, she wired her mother: OKAY

VISIT MURIEL SENDING CHECK CARE HER DONT WORRY ABOUT RACE....-AE.

The "Powder Puff Derby," as the newspapers named it, originated two days later from Clover Field in Santa Monica. Eight days were allotted for the twenty women pilots to fly the course to Cleveland, Ohio, and the race would terminate with a first prize of $2500. Amelia was dead serious as she listened to Master of Ceremonies Will Rogers refer to the entrants as "ladybirds" and "flying flappers." Although he would later become a close friend, at the moment Amelia saw no humor in his remarks. She was setting out with her sisters to prove they could meet the test of capability in the air.

Among the pilots were Amelia's friendly competitors, Ruth Nichols, Louise Thaden, and Blanche Noyes, who were also impatient to be in the air. They took off at one-minute intervals and all made it safely to San Bernardino, sixty miles to the east, for the first night. Subsequently Amelia damaged her propeller at Yuma, Arizona, Blanche ground-looped at Pecos, Texas, and Marvel Crosson was killed at Phoenix. On the seventh day, Amelia and Ruth Nichols were leading in elapsed time, but when Ruth's plane crashed at the end of the runway and Amelia ran to pull her friend out of the wreckage, she lost her turn to take off. Louise Thaden was first into Cleveland, Gladys O'Donnell was second, and Amelia came in third. More important to the women, the race assured their future acceptance in aviation.

In October Mrs. Earhart was visiting her sister in Germantown, Pennsylvania, when Amelia wired her from St. Louis. PROBABLY HOME SUNDAY FOR ONE DAY...The following month she and a number of other women flyers met at Curtiss-Wright Field, and although the founding of the Ninety-Nines, an association of women pilots, has been attributed by the legend mostly to Amelia, records show that at least four of the ninety-nine charter members, and probably more, participated in forming the organization. Three weeks later she was in Los Angeles again. Between the telegram and the following letter, she had not seen her mother.

Amelia Earhart. Self-portrait. Date uncertain.

Amy Otis Earhart and Edwin Stanton Earhart. 1895.

Amelia and friends at a Fourth of July tea party. Kansas City. 1904.

(Photo by Golling)

Amelia Earhart. St. Paul. 1914.

As a volunteer nurse. Toronto. 1917.

Muriel and Amelia Earhart. Santa Monica. 1923.

With Sam Chapman. Los Angeles. 1923.

(*Paramount News*)

Revving up propeller. Los Angeles. 1921.

Training plane. Boston. 1926.

Group portrait of the Ninety-Nines. AE fourth from right. 1929.

Seated in her Lockheed Vega. 1930.

Greeted by the Mayor of Southampton after transatlantic flight on
Friendship. 1928.

Amelia Earhart and her mother. North Hollywood. 1932.

Los Angeles, [November 22, 1929]

Dear Mammy,

I too must write in pencil for there is no ink available. I have been having a lovely time here flying a great deal. Today I think I broke the women's speed record in average time of 184.17 m.p.h. I did one lap in 197+.

N.A. [Nora Alstulund, AE's secretary] is here with me at the Madduxes. The Lindberghs haven't yet arrived but are expected soon.

I have to make a trip east to Omaha on the second but will return here before coming to New York again. In the new arrangement I am half time with both eastern and western divisions of T.A.T.

Cousin Rilla [Challiss] called me yesterday but left in evening so I didn't see her. I was busy the whole day in the speed trials.

I haven't seen Dad yet but expect to tomorrow...

I certainly like this country and do not like the thot of coming east. I'll try to write you again soon.

A.E.

Amelia did go to see Edwin, who was living with his second wife Helen, in a cabin on five acres of land in Eagle Rock, a short distance north of Los Angeles. She found her father probably happier than he had ever been but not well. As she wrote to Muriel, "I'm afraid Dad may not enjoy his little cabin too long, Pidge...He looks thinner than I've ever seen him, and Helen says he has no appetite at all and tires very quickly now." He was also "long on friends but short of cash," as he told Amelia, and he was worried about being able to make his mortgage payment. She paid off the mortgage, about $2000, and arranged a life tenancy freehold which would give the property to her father and after his death to his widow. Title of the property remained in her own name and she designated Muriel as her ultimate heir, after Amy.

Los Angeles, [undated]

Dear Mother,

By all means stay with Pidge [in her first pregnancy]. I think she needs you and apparently Albert is no judge. Keep out of his way and disappear when he is about. Poor old Sis. I'm sorry she's having so much rotten luck.

I don't think I shall be here much longer. I must return to New York...before Christmas — unless it rains out here. I am flying a good deal and think carrying on work as well here for the time as in New York.

I went to Omaha to make a speech for the Pennsylvania Railroad and turned about and came back. On the way I stopped over night at Tucson to see Porter Adams who is there at a sanatorium. Who should be there too but Mrs. Silliman. I didn't remember her from Adam but I suppose she is Bliss Wise and Silliman, isn't she?

I am glad my article in the Federated News got publicity in Boston. It did in Washington, too, and other places.

Nora is taking these out to mail so I'll write you later...

A.E.

The article concerned putting the names of towns on roofs for the aid of pilots in locating themselves. Amelia had appealed to the 14,000 members of the General Federation of Women's Clubs. "Surprising as it may seem many cities in the same geographical region look very much alike from a few thousand feet up," she wrote, and advocated painting the name in the "largest possible letters on the roof of the largest building."

Los Angeles, [December 18, 1929]

Dear Mammy,

Horray for Chrizmuzz. Here's something for you and

Pidge. I can't make it in time I think, but will probably arrive for a while shortly after.

How's Pidge? I hope she's feeling better.

Let me know when you are short and I'll send along
some cash.

Goo' bye

A.E.

The year 1929 marked a turning point in Amelia's life. Her
future was now committed to aviation, and she would do everything she could for her family, but at a remove. The separation
was not deep, not deliberate, and certainly not complete, but the
distinctions were there. The AE of the legend, the professional
woman, would live publicly; the daughter and sister would live
mostly in the past and in letters to and from her mother and
sister which maintained but did not depend on the familial connections; and the private woman would live alone and apart as
she always had, proudly, independently, sometimes secretly, and
always honestly.

George Palmer Putnam had reached a crucial moment also.
When his divorce from Dorothy became final on December 20,
he made the first of five proposals of marriage. Amelia turned
him down.

TEN

Father's Death
1930

Amelia Earhart was not only intensely feminine, she was an intense feminist who hoped for a day when "women will know no restrictions because of sex, but will be individuals free to live their lives as men are free..." Freedom to her meant flying when and where she wanted to without a husband and children waiting at home to make conventional demands on her time and energy. She liked men and enjoyed both professional and personal association with many, but she valued her own independence more.

Five times she refused GP because, as she wrote to a friend, she was "unsold on marriage." She thought she might never be able to see it "except as a cage until I am unfit to work or fly or be active — and of course I wouldn't be attractive then..." Nevertheless, she must have considered it each time GP asked her, and in between when she read impudent speculation in the gossip columns. In an undated note to Amy she stated her position:

> Dear Mother,
>   ...I shall not stay in New York very long I think as I am going west again to pick up my ship. There are several dates in Middle West I must keep too...
>   I am not marrying *anybody*.
>   A.E.

The courtship was not easy, according to GP, who reported in *Soaring Wings* that he wrote to Amelia frequently and in reply received only notes in the margins of his long letters. Both were involved in a number of projects, separated more often than not, and able to converse only briefly in Amelia's office at *Cosmopolitan*, or for a few minutes in passing before her takeoff or his in whatever airport they happened to meet.

In addition to work and her private affairs, Amelia was busy arranging financial security for her mother:

New York, [February 3, 1930]

Dear Mother,

I am enclosing a check for $100. Hereafter you will receive it monthly from the Fifth Avenue Bank. I have put all my earnings into stocks and bonds and the yearly income in your name. The list includes the $1000 bond of yours which you may have, of course, at any time. I also have you down as beneficiary of a small fraternal accident endowment which you will receive in case I pop off. This through the National Air Pilots Association of Cleveland.

[Nora Alstulund] and I are living together in a large double room at about half the rent of the suite. I am thus able to live easily on what I make and you may have the other.

I sent the clothing on because I thot it would please Pidge and was probably needed. . .Please let me know how she is.

I have just returned from Washington and Pittsburgh and am off again to the west soon.

I now have a [public relations] job with the Pennsylvania R.R. besides T.A.T. Maddux. I plan to work very hard this year and little else but fly.

I'll write you again soon.

A.E.

Los Angeles, [February 18, 1930]

Dear Mammy,

I saw a lil dress and bought it for you. I hope it fits.

It is so hot here I can only think of summer.

Came unexpectedly from Albuquerque as I found something wrong with the plane. I had again hoped to hop off yesterday or today and now I find my departure will be tomorrow morning.

I wish I could stay here.

A.E.

Saw Dad yesterday. He has been ill.

Edwin was suffering from stomach cancer, as yet undiagnosed. Amelia found him even thinner than he had been the previous fall, but she saw no reason to burden her mother with details. Even as late as September 1930, less than a month before he died, Amelia thought the condition was a stricture of the esophagus.

In the meantime, Mrs. Earhart had responded with objections to the financial help Amelia had arranged for her.

New York, [February 25, 1930]

Dear Mother,

Please do not think you are taking my hard earned cash (even tho I would give it willingly.)

What you receive comes from what the cash receives from being put into bonds etc. And that is extra to what I earn. I am living with Nora and very economically so there will be more and more accruing.

I wrote you from California and sent a small surprise which you should have. I shall get up to Boston sometime during the month.

A.E.

The visit home had to be postponed. Gene Vidal and Paul Collins had left TAT, and with Amelia as vice president were in the middle of forming the New York, Philadelphia and Washington Airway Corporation. Scheduled to open on September 1, 1930, the organization planned ten round-trip flights at hourly intervals to the three cities. Amelia believed it to be the "first really frequent service in the world."

New York, [March 6, 1930]

Dear Mommie,

Many happies! [Amy's birthday, March 7] I have ordered you some A.O.E. stationery which isn't ready yet but will be soon. Also I am sending a lil package which I hope you'll like. The salts will have to do for the actual date, for I fear the other may not reach you by tomorrow...

Also a coupla dollies for a little thing you may want — maybe a swell show at the local movie palace or a book. By the way shall I send you Nat. Geog. or do you get [it] regularly?

Love
A.E.

New York, [March 19, 1930]

Dear Mother,

Enclosed is the check. There was an important meeting of 28 women pilots on Sat. and Sunday. We (three or four of them) worked on minutes etc. and I couldn't come. I am planning definitely to leave here Friday night. I'll wire you when I'll arrive.

Hastily,
A.E.

The meeting was held to continue planning for the Ninety-Nines, the organization which had originated the previous November. Amelia was elected the first president, and Louise Thaden became the first secretary. The purpose was for fellowship, to aid in securing jobs for women, and to keep records on women pilots.

Behind the constant pressures of her public and private life, Amelia dreamed about a notable flight for herself. When a friend suggested the possibility of a solo transatlantic crossing, however, she said, "I admit I should like to do it, but I know it would be foolhardy for me to attempt it until I've had considerably more flying and navigation experience. Give me say, eighteen months to two years and then we'll see."

Everywhere she went, people asked her plans, and rumors of a flight followed her like hounds on a scent. She denied these with a straight face, and went quietly about preparing herself for the venture. With Dr. James H. Kimball — the New York meteorologist who had given weather reports for the 1928 transatlantic flight — she studied weather and weather patterns, learning the significance of "barometric pressures, wind direction and velocity, visibility and temperature, and whether rain, snow, fog or sunshine prevailed" at any of many points in the United States and over the Atlantic. Watching as he penciled in isobars and isotherms, she could talk freely in the language they both understood. Along with Commander Byrd, Bernt Balchen, Colonel Lindbergh, Ruth Elder, and others, Amelia depended on "Doc" for the success of her flights.

New York, May 26, 1930

Dear Mother,

I arrived in Philadelphia the other day and called the [Balis] family residence only to find you had left a few hours earlier. I am sorry we missed each other on our hurried trips. I haven't heard recently how Auntie [Amy's sister Margaret] is, but cannot see how there is much chance...

I hope Pidge is feeling better. I'll try to get up there as soon as I can for a short visit, though I can't say definitely when that will be.

L.O.L.

A.E.

After Mrs. Earhart wrote to Edwin announcing the birth of Muriel's son David Morrissey, he responded with a friendly letter saying he was pleased to be a granddad. He noted that when Amelia was in Los Angeles, he did not see much of her, but he did follow her around in the newspapers. He remarked that he was very much better, not admitting that his condition was really much worse.

> Detroit, Michigan
> June 28, 1930
>
> Dear Mother,
> Dad is ill. He will have to undergo an operation for some stricture of the esophagus. Of course I'll have to stand the expense and will gladly but I wish I knew who the physician is and something about him. I have written Mrs. [Helen] Earhart to find out more about the situation.
> I am in Detroit trying some speed runs and have been so delayed that my [plan?] to come to Marblehead has not been possible.
> Thank Pidge for her wire and tell her I'll write her later. I hope she and Rastus [David] are well.
> Let me know if there's anything you need, etc.
> A.E.

On that same day, Amelia had broken the speed records for 100 kilometers, and 100 kilometers with a payload of 500 kilograms, in her new Lockheed Vega purchased after the sale of the Avian Moth. When she returned to New York, she found a letter from her father.

> Eagle Rock, California
> June 27, 1930
>
> Dear Mill:
> Your kindly letter at hand. I would like to follow the suggestions, but cannot. I see Dr. Hensley this

afternoon. I am far too weak for an operation at present, and have been advised to go into a sanitarium to recuperate and gain some flesh and strength as I weigh only 105 pounds...

I tried two hospitals but I was confronted with a stiff entrance fee and...I did not want to undergo the embarrassment and publicity of asking them to send the bills to you.

Meantime I now expect to realize some money on one of my cases within the next week or so. I also have a line on a surgeon who worked with Dr. Jenkins in New York who makes a speciality of dilating wind-pipes...

I will investigate this...[but] am going to do every thing I can to avoid an operation as I am very fearful of the consequences. In any event, I am going to put it off as long as possible...

I thank you very much for your offer and your letter.

Sincerely,
Dad

On the back, Amelia scribbled, "Am heading West and will see him there," and then forwarded her father's letter to Amy, in Philadelphia with the Balis family.

New York, August 8, 1930

Dear Mother,

I have been so rushed since returning from the coast I haven't looked up from my desk. I am as you know trying to help in starting a new airline. It is to be opened Sept. 1 and there are 1000000 things to do.

I saw Dad on the coast. He is desperately ill — starving to death. There is a stricture of some kind which prevents his taking much nourishment. His mind is clear and he says he's better...Mrs. Earhart is almost breaking under the strain so I said I'd help out in monthly payments so she could rest. . .

I haven't heard since your last letter about Auntie.

I'm fairly well but have to stick on the job pretty strenuously. I am disappointed about not getting up to see you but I've been away. How long do you remain in Mizzlerhead? Maybe I can make it yet for I'm not going into races this year. . .

Lemme know how Pidge and you are. It's actually warm in the city, but I don't mind heat fortunately.

The only thing I've done here is to see Lysistrata and it was good.

A.E.

In answer to a letter of inquiry from Muriel, Dr. C. M. Hensley of Eagle Rock replied on September 3 that Edwin's condition was cancer of the stomach. He explained that an operation would only hasten death, and added that the outlook was grave and there was "little hope for his recovery. . ."

Later the same day, Dr. Hensley wired Amelia: BLOOD TRANS-FUSION ABSOLUTELY NECESSARY FOR FATHER COST ONE HUNDRED SEVENTY FIVE DOLLARS WILL YOU GUARANTEE BILL FOR THE ABOVE AMOUNT LATER REPLY. Amelia penciled on the bottom of the telegram, "Of course I guaranteed," and sent it to her mother.

New York, [September 16, 1930]

Dear Mother,

I am sorry I haven't answered your letter before but I have been and am terribly occupied with the infant airline.

I received a telegram from Dr. Hensley saying I must come soon. Also Mrs. E. wired that Dad was perfectly rational and anxious to see me. It is so hard to get away so expensive, that I am almost staggered with the thot of going west. However I feel I must grant [his] wish and will probably shove off tomorrow. One thing he is not suffering. I can't believe it's cancer therefore. I suppose he is too weak for an operation but it seems as if I'd prefer that risk than starving as he is now.

I fear I shan't be able to get north. I've tried and planned so often and then find myself stuck on the job here...

I do hope Pidge moves out of her hole. I feel as you do it's bad for health and morale. All the middle-classness of the family heritage bursts into bloom in such surroundings. All the fineness — for there's some — is squashed. It would be unless you were around.

These are sad times. I'll write again soon.

A.

Amelia spent nearly a week with Edwin and Helen Earhart in Eagle Rock and believed her father was much improved. She started for New York on Tuesday, September 23, only to turn around when Mrs. Earhart wired her at Tucson. Edwin had died about eight hours after Amelia left the house. Following the funeral in California, Amelia returned to New York, and almost without stopping hurried to keep a lecture engagement before the Traffic Club in Norfolk, Virginia.

New York, [October 2, 1930]

Dear Mother,

Your letter [from Germantown] saved my sending the check to Beantown.

I just returned from Dad to have a little crackup due to a mechanical failure. The lock on the pilot's cockpit opened and let me out as I was leaning against it. I wasn't hurt much and neither was Lockheed.

About Dad. The diagnosis was correct. When he had the haemorage [sic] the doctor said he practically knew. Of course Dad didn't and Helen Earhart said the improvement was so marked for a time she didn't believe it. However, he waged a hopeless fight against a thing which took all his nourishment. He grew thinner and thinner and waited for me to come and change doctors or get him to a sanitarium or change diet because he didn't want to go. I tried and had x-rays to please him, and he hoped until he could not move his poor hands. He didn't miss [me] when I left as we gave morphine at the last so he wouldn't worry about [my] leaving.

His big case was lost and we told him he won. He couldn't have stood the disappointment so it was for the best.

I wrote up the little history and paid the hundred little debts he always had. Stationery, etc. — you know.

He asked about you and Pidge a lot, and I faked telegrams for him from you all. He was an aristocrat as he went — all the weaknesses gone with a little boy's brown puzzled eyes.

I'll try to get to Phila. to see you if you'll let me know the situation there. I am full of anti-tetanus serum so not feeling quite up to snuff. N.A.'s on her vacation for a week.

A.E.

Any guilt concerning the adolescent hurts she had inflicted on Edwin was now canceled. Her presence at his side, her time and her money to calm his mind and ease his passing, her provision for his widow, and even her faking telegrams from Amy and Muriel may have been subconscious acts of atonement. Now for what she had done, or had not done, past or present, she had no regrets.

The realization left Amelia unaccustomedly uneasy and at a loose end. Also she was not really well as she had noted in August. Since then her father's illness, plus all the other family troubles, had added to the stress and constant pressure of her work. Because cockpits were not yet enclosed, she probably was again suffering from sinusitis aggravated by the antitetanus shot. Understandably her resistance was low, and her health "not quite up to snuff."

She was at another crossroad. Ahead she saw only one more business conference to attend, one more hurried journey to make, one more lecture to give, one more letter or article to write, one more strange hand to shake, and many others to dodge. But what else?

Although she would be alone all her life, no matter in what company, she could not shake off an unusual and infrequent sense of depression and aloneness, which others might have called loneliness. Oddest of all, she had a desire to go home, even though home had never been in Eagle Rock with Edwin and Helen Earhart, nor could it be any longer with Amy, who divided her time between the Morrissey family in Medford and Philadelphia where her sister was terminally ill. Home could hardly be one room in a woman's hotel shared with her secretary in New York City.

Home with Sam Chapman? Marriage at the expense of aviation? Sam, patient and loyal, utterly devoted, why didn't he see that the only way to keep Amelia Earhart was to let her go? No, not marriage with Sam. Marriage with anyone else? A man who not only would let her go but would find the money for her journeying?

Late in the fall, at the Burbank Lockheed factory, when George Putnam made his sixth proposal of marriage, Amelia casually patted his arm and accepted.

ELEVEN

Rye, New York 1930-1931

The engagement was not announced, and no wedding date was set. Above everything, Amelia wanted no publicity, and in this George indulged her, possibly fearing if he didn't she would call it all off.

As vice president of the New York, Philadelphia and Washington Airway Corporation, Amelia was required to travel more than before, to deal with complaints and explain to the public how it was impossible to fit eleven passengers into a plane designed to carry ten, to write endless letters and make innumerable speeches, all designed to advertise the new service. In addition, she had her own schedules to keep, her own articles to write, her own fan mail, huge lots of it, to answer.

She usually enclosed a letter or note with her monthly check to Amy, but aside from family news, money and clothing sometimes seemed to be all she wrote about.

New York, [October 13, 1930]

Dear Mother,

I don't quite know where you are as I had a package containing Christine [sic] Lavransdatter from Medford addressed in your handwriting. This goes to Philadelphia nevertheless.

In sending your check last month, I forgot to tell

101

you that the money is for you. I know how easy it is for you to give it away to Pidge and the Balises. However I am not working to support either. Little things are all right but I don't want any large proportion to get out of your hands — borrowed or given.

The line is turning out very well so far. We have carried more than 5000 passengers in the first thirty days. Did Emily [Balis?] ever get her ride to Atlantic City? I had tickets sent to the house and hope she went. Uncle Clarence objected strenuously at the mention of her going but I sent the wherewithal anyway.

How is Auntie? It seems such a shame to linger on and on when there is no hope.

I don't know when I shall get over to Phila for a visit. I come over fairly often on business...

A

New York, [December 31, 1930]

Dear Mother,

I sent you two pkgs. yesterday. They're Chrizmuz surprizes. Please go to a decent tailor and have the brown suit fitted. I think it won't need much. Take Nancy [Balis] with you and get it done right. The blouse will probably be too large for you, but [I'll] try to send another one along anyway. I have another thing for you too, which I'll shoot over soon as I can.

I want you to go to town with Nancy and buy a lil brown hat to go with suit (a shade or two darker maybe) and a couple of prs. gloves for it if needed. Then while you're at it get a dark blue hat — something like black one you bot yourself last year. Charge these to Balis acct. and send me the bill. Take Nancy to luncheon and show if you wish. I'll send you regular check after first.

I sent Pidge some undies and small check. She seems cheerful.

Expect to be Phila. soon but never know when, and [am] all around when there.

L.O.L.

A

Mrs. Earhart remained with the Balis family in Philadelphia over the holidays, and on January 4, 1931, her sister died.

Washington, [January 19, 1931]

Dear Momie,

I am very sorry to have been remisser than usual in my correspondence. I have spent much time in Wash and way stations and have been very busy.

Your telegram about Aunty did not reach me until after the funeral. I felt you would call on me for any-thing needed so did not write.

I have been in Phila. now and then but always in a rush of business. I haven't called because it seemed so inevitable a thing that enquiry would be almost un-wanted. I'll drop in somehow if you think I should.

What is happening in the family?...I got word [Pidge] and Albert had found a house to buy. They need some money to help out. I have written asking about details and may ask you to go up and give your judgment. If she hasn't mentioned it to you don't say anything. By the way maybe the other thing [Muriel's second pregnancy] is not positive. I haven't exact dope.

I am on board a P.R.R. train just pulling into Wash-ington. The planes didn't fly today and I had to be present at a contest committee meeting tomorrow...

Speaking of relatives, Toot is in Calif. now and some-one who calls himself Cram Earhart writes me to visit them in Florida.

A

At some time or other, Amelia found a moment, either in

person or by telephone, to tell her mother she was engaged to George Palmer Putnam. Amy opposed the marriage; not only was GP twelve years older, he was a divorced man, reason enough for one of her generation to rule him out for her daughter. Perhaps she had another reason. Later she would remark that "We neither of us had much time for confidential talks because of schedules and things. It was utterly impossible and I reached a stage where I felt the only time I had a chance to talk to her was when I was holding on to her coat tails." Probably she resented the prospect of sharing AE's already limited attention with a man who continued to address her as Mrs. Earhart until after Amelia disappeared in 1937, when she suddenly became "Dear Mother Earhart."

Whatever the truth, her objections had no influence on Amelia.

>New York, [February 4, 1931]
>
>Dear Momie,
>
>   I shant be home over this next weekend. Why don't you plan your and [Balis] girls trip for next one. Of course if you wish, come anyway, and [Nora] can attend details of rooms, etc.
>
>   I am due in Wash. tonight and have a luncheon in Newark today.
>
>Cheerio,
>
>A

Three days later, on February 7, Amelia Mary Earhart and George Palmer Putnam were married at his mother's house in Noank, Connecticut. Obviously Amelia was still "unsold on marriage," for the morning of the wedding, she handed her fiancé an extraordinary letter, which he termed "brutal in its frankness but beautiful in its honesty."

>Dear GP,
>
>   There are some things which should be writ before

we are married. Things we have talked over before, — most of them.

You must know again my reluctance to marry, my feeling that I shatter thereby chances in work which means so much to me. I feel the move just now as foolish as anything I could do. I know there may be compensations, but have no heart to look ahead.

In our life together I shall not hold you to any medieval code of faithfulness to me, nor shall I consider myself bound to you similarly. If we can be honest I think the differences which arise may best be avoided.

Please let us not interfere with each other's work or play, nor let the world see private joys or disagreements. In this connection I may have to keep some place where I can go to be myself now and then, for I cannot guarantee to endure at all times the confinements of even an attractive cage.

I must exact a cruel promise, and this is that you will let me go in a year if we find no happiness together.

I will try to do my best in every way.

A.E.

Hatless and dressed in a slightly worn brown suit, with a crepe blouse and brown shoes, Amelia must have kept her hands still and her face averted as her bridegroom read the letter. Understanding that most men would recoil from the prospect of marriage on those terms, she was prepared for refusal from George and perhaps eager for it. Still, she was also prepared to enter this marriage and make it a working partnership, never letting her end of the bargain down. She would never have come so far if she hadn't already squared her conscience by announcing honestly her intention to be free of "any medieval code of faithfulness."

George probably was not in love with Amelia, but he was certain of the value for him in any marriage arrangement he could persuade her to accept, even at the cost of male pride and surrender of male prerogatives in the home. After reading her letter, he only smiled and nodded. Then he took her hand and the ceremony proceeded.

The new Mrs. Putnam's first act after her wedding was to wire her sister Muriel: OVER THE BROOMSTICK WITH GP TODAY STOP BREAK NEWS GENTLY TO MOTHER. She signed it A.E., and she did not herself thereafter use her husband's name if she could avoid it.

Reporters swarmed around the senior Mrs. Putnam's house, and GP dealt handily with them, telling them more than they wanted to know and much less than they expected. He had every intention of allowing Amelia to run her life as she wished; the only change he made was to arrange his own affairs differently from before. He sold his share of G. P. Putnam's Sons to a cousin, and became head of the editorial department for Paramount Pictures. Subject only to appearing at story conferences, he made himself free to tag along after his wife.

In Philadelphia, when news of the marriage broke, reporters found Mrs. Earhart staying at the Balis residence. MARRIAGE PLEASES AMELIA'S MOTHER ran the headline under a morgue photo of Amy and Muriel together, and Amy was quoted as saying, "If Amelia is happy, and I am sure she is, then I am. I knew it was to take place of course, and I know Mr. Putnam very well. But I didn't know the exact date of it."

Amy Otis Earhart was now in her sixties, living a quiet life and helping any relative who might need money, a homemaker, or a friendly shoulder to cry on. The reporters found her as "blue-eyed, slender and erect of carriage" as Amelia, only not as tall. She was devoted to her daughters and grandchildren, and if she didn't like Amelia's marriage, she was too much a lady ever to admit it to the press.

New York, [February 22, 1931]

Dear Mother,

I want you to know I appreciate more than I can say the interview you gave in Phila. about my marriage. I was so proud of you.

I am much happier than I expected I could ever be in that state. I believe the whole thing was for the best. Of course I go on in the same way as before as far as business is concerned. I haven't changed at all and will only be busier I suppose...

I want you to come over as soon as you wish and see the apartment [at 42 West 58th Street]. I have two canaries and you know I've wanted one for ever so long. You can stay here at the hotel in another room. If the cousins want to come they can be here too...

I sent Muriel the $2500 promised. I hope it will mean a lot to her, moving into a decent house. I can't see Medford anywhere, however, with Albert's biz in Cambridge, etc. When are you going there, do you know? I am asking Pidge down here, maybe we could have a blowout together before she becomes tied down — or is it obviously too late for her?

Write me your plans.

Yr. doter,

A

Another extraordinary letter. Amelia made no mention of her husband, but said she was happier than she had expected to be. Still, after only two weeks of marriage, to invite her mother and cousins as well as her pregnant sister to visit is not the usual bridal behavior. But Amelia was not the usual bride, and as expected, she did become busier than before. In fact, there had been no time for a honeymoon. Almost at once, the couple was absorbed in what AE called their "solo jobs."

New York, [March 6, 1931]

Dear Mother,

I sent you a little blue suit for your birfday. It was late but I wasn't sure of the new address so held it over.

Please have the little tailor in So. Medford fix it for you and I'll send you a shirt to wear with.

I'll try to come up sometime and pick out what I
want. I'd like the old music books sent down now if
you can ship them. Also the green set of modern music.
As to blankets give those to Pidge. I should like the
old quilts etc and the things which were grandma's.
Of course the old set will be marked for you in case
I pop off. Everything I have in fact.

Sam [Chapman] has been here all afternoon. It was
good seeing him and we had a swell time.

I'll write you again soon as I must dress for dinner
now.

A

Along with her other activities, AE was now seriously involved
with an autogiro. In the previous December she had made a flight
in preparation for a *Cosmopolitan* article, and as she admitted in
The Fun of It, she didn't know "whether I flew it, or it flew me."
Now she set out to prove women could safely fly a "round-wing"
airplane.

On April 8, at Pitcairn Field in Willow Grove, Pennsylvania,
with a barograph installed by the National Aeronautic Association, she achieved an altitude record, carrying an oxygen bottle
with her to 15,000 feet where her engine faltered. It recovered,
and she managed to attain 18,000 feet before she was blown east
of the test area and had to come down. She had not used the
oxygen because her lungs "did the job unassisted." Later that same
day, she broke her own first record by flying to 18,415 feet.

Her ability to handle the machine led to a cross-country hop
to advertise the Beech-Nut Packing Corporation. AE's own reason for accepting the commission was to know for herself what
the autogiro could do and what its future might be. Only a dozen
years old at the time, the round-wing plane would later be called
a helicopter, and its functions extended far beyond the sightseeing
tours over Washington, D.C., that Amelia envisioned for it.

Before her departure for the West Coast, however, she underwent minor surgery, possibly the removal of her tonsils, which she mentioned in a letter to her mother.

>   New York, [April 27, 1931]
> Dear Mrs. Eho
>   I'm home now but almost inarticulate. Also the knees are a bit wobbly. The job was very thoroughly done so the mending will be a little drawn out. Then age makes a difference too. I remember Pidge's trial at Worthington and believe children have the advantage.
>   Thank you for sending the music boogs. I remembered three and you sent two of Grandma's only. Am I wrong? The old poetry is swell too. How is your stationery holding out? Let me know when it gets low. And what else do you need?
>   Please have Muriel send me a properly drawn second mortgage. I suppose it is impossible to impress upon her the fact that [a] businesslike relationship between relatives is not an unfriendly act. Where others [are] involved clean cut understanding should obtain. I'm no Scrooge to ask that some acknowledgement of a twentyfive hundred dollar loan be given me. I work hard for my money. Whether or not I shall exact repayment is my business, nevertheless Pidge should feel some responsibility for protecting me against the loss of that sum. You understand but I think she never will...Suppose she and Albert pop off tomorrow? I'd have no claim on the property at all, and would probably have to sue Mrs. Morrissey or some other old Turk.
>   Cheerio anyway,
>   Yr. Doter.

If the sisters physically resembled each other, their life styles were totally different. Rye, with its old-family history, its estates and Westchester County social reputation, was nothing at all like

Medford, north of Boston on the Mystic River. The town was settled in 1630, and Paul Revere galloped through it on the road to Lexington one midnight in 1775. A former shipbuilding center, famous for its rum, it was an industrial town in 1931, a source of paper boxes, metal products and chemicals, bricks and calico. It had a town square, some ancient clapboard houses, a public library, Tufts University, and on the High Street the Episcopal Grace Church.

Unless Amelia was making spectacular news, the Morrisseys and Mrs. Earhart drew no more than ordinary attention. The family attended church on Sunday, Albert went daily to work in Cambridge, Mrs. Earhart minded her grandson and kept house, and Muriel taught at the Grace Church Day School, earning four or five extra dollars a week to put with what Albert gave her each month for all expenses.

"If I were made differently, I suppose I would save first and not have to pay back later," Pidge would wail to her mother in a 1941 letter. But this was ten years earlier, and Mrs. Earhart was right there in the house, secretly handing over a dollar here or five there in spite of Amelia's displeasure with the practice. Albert had no idea of this, but Muriel, who was pregnant for the second time, "didn't know what [she'd] do without it."

At the Grace Church Day School, she had charge of Grade I, and in addition she canvassed the parish for more students, helped transport the kindergartners, directed dramatic programs for holidays, and spent hours grading papers and filling out diplomas when the school term ended. She liked the work and believed she was good at it. Those with whom she worked agreed, and everyone said that she and her mother were two of the nicest women God ever made. The sister, the flyer, well, they didn't see much of Amelia, but Mrs. Morrissey and Mrs. Earhart, they were angels.

Unfortunately the family problem was Albert. Who knows why a man fails to take responsibility for his family? Why he refuses to do anything at all for his own mother, ignores his children, and sometimes won't speak to his wife for weeks on end? Perhaps Albert felt trapped by the marriage, perhaps he knew about the "family failing," as Amelia called her mother's way of handing out money. Whatever the reason, there was always money for American Legion dues and donations, or for a new uniform, but he gave his wife only seventy-five dollars a month for house payment, heat, light, food, telephone, dentist and doctor, clothing for the family, Christmas and birthday gifts, church dues, parish suppers, and any recreation she could manage. By scrounging here and there, by paying the grocery bill one month and letting it go the next in favor of paying her life insurance premiums, Muriel managed to maintain policies destined to pay for the children's college education and almost entirely to repay Amelia for the house loan.

The residence at 118 Traincroft Avenue was situated up a hill from the town square and it was large, with an attic and a cellar. Mrs. Earhart had a bedroom to herself, and the children had theirs. Downstairs in the living room was a green Wilton rug which Amy had hung on to over the years, a piano, side tables, and comfortable chairs. In the dining room stood Great Grandmother Harres's precious sideboard. If sometimes the family all had colds because the heat was kept so low, at least the house was usually presentable for callers, although Muriel hesitated to invite family or friends because of Albert's uncertain temper. And she would have died if the town knew how poorly the Morrisseys really lived. Amy was her only support, and her son her only joy.

Absorbed in the coming birth of her second child, her homely pursuits, and her school, in church service and counting pennies at home, Muriel hardly stopped to think about Amelia and her activities. On May 29, 1931, she heard a radio broadcast saying her sister had taken off from Newark for the West Coast in the Beech-Nut autogiro.

TWELVE

AE and GP
1931-1932

Amelia flew the northern mail route to Oakland, California, where she landed on June 6, only the second autogiro ever to land there. She started back from Los Angeles and arrived safely in Abilene, Texas, but crashed on takeoff. This led to a letter of reprimand from the Department of Commerce, delivered to her at Tulsa, Oklahoma, where she was lecturing. News reports said she had been "careless and used bad judgment," but in *Soaring Wings* her husband quoted her as saying, "We'd have made it but for the crowd...I was afraid a child might run out suddenly or we might hit a car...I did what I thought was best in the circumstances."

On June 22 she returned to Newark, having traveled 11,000 miles in the autogiro but spending only 150 hours in the air to do it. From the airport she went straight to the spacious Putnam house in Rye, twenty-four miles northeast of New York City. Founded in 1660, the town had a fine beach on Long Island Sound and many large estates among the old oaks and elm trees. Amelia not only fitted into the setting, she had loved the sixteen-room house when she first saw it in 1928. Now she was ready to put her own imprint on the long, low-studded building in its clump of old shade trees where pink and white dogwood bloomed in the spring.

The Putnam family was represented in the American Revolution by two generals, and in 1848 the first George Palmer Putnam had founded the publishing firm which still bears his name. He was a founder and honorary superintendent of the Metropolitan Museum of Art, and one of his sons became Librarian of Congress. The other carried on the publishing firm until he was succeeded by his son, the second George Palmer Putnam, who sold it when he married AE.

Whatever changes Amelia made in the Rye house were probably inconspicuous. In time, it became a place of reunion for her and GP, of entertaining celebrated friends, and riding or swimming with GP's young sons when they visited from Florida.

Rye, [June 27, 1931]

Dear Mrs. Eho,

I have been away as you no doubt have saw by the infallible press. I had a very interesting trip in a still experimental plane, and I come home with a sunburned nose as memento. I got your letter along the way, but had no chance to answer it before this date. I don't know when I can come north. I have tried and tried, but the time now seems several weeks ahead.

Why can't you come here for a few days visit? I'd love to show you the place and there would be nothing but whatever we wanted to do. I'm busy part of the day. However I am sure you would be comfortable here and find much you could do if you wished. I have various housekeeping probs I should like to refer to you, such as, "What makes sheets smell musty?" etc. I think Pidge could spare you for a lil while and mebbe you need the rest before the second coming, if I may put it that way. I have so much and would like to share what I have with my mama, now and again. Lemme know soon, telegram tomorro. I'm sending you a package Sat or Mon.

L.O.L.
A.E.

Rye, [July, 1931]

Dear Mammy,

Here are two checks a dol or more short. I'll make the difference up next month as I haven't my check boog along.

The dress is for you. I don't know what Pidge needs or wants. If there are some little things she ought to have lemme know. I imagine you spend most of your money on her or Thee [Theodore Harres Otis, Amy's youngest brother] so prefer to send stuff to you. I know you don't get anything for yourself...

The [Department of Commerce] reprimand wasn't one really...I am not a careless pilot and the letter doesn't say so. It came 10 days after the news release.

As I told you, I'm at Rye for the summer — Locust Ave., no number. If you get around to shipping any silver or the walnut table send there. I'm afraid to have the old vases shipped.

I didn't realize Pidge was so near. I certainly hope she makes it as easily as possible. Also that she has learned enough about anatomy to prevent further trials for a while.

A.

Amelia apparently liked children and might have had her own in time, but for now, pregnancy was an inconvenience, a "trial" she had no desire to undergo. She once told Muriel it "took too long to make a baby." An instinct unfulfilled, however, could possibly explain why she treated her mother as an irresponsible child at times, and why she was critical of what she saw as "rough spots" in her sister's marriage. On the other hand, she may only have been hurt that Mrs. Earhart failed to accept this first invitation to Rye after the marriage.

Rye, [July 14, 1931]

Dear Mother,

I found the walnut table here. I didn't recognize it and wasn't present at the opening to see it unpacked.

Don't send breakables like the old vases — just silver and boogs. I'd love the old Pucks and Dr. Syntax that Pidge never cared about.

Hope she's o.k.

I do wish you could get away a few days to visit here. Maybe if I got in a helper you could.

How about looking for one there in case.

A.

[Postmarked] August 4, 1931

Hey, Hey,

The candlesticks were sweet. I've had 'em on the table ever since they came. I hope you'll come and look at them.

How's Pidge? I've been expecting word about her any day.

The silver and linen arrived O.K. and I was glad to get. I haven't opened the books yet as I have to clear spaces to put them in.

A.E.

In the middle of the month Amelia went to Boston to visit Muriel and the new baby girl born on July 31 and named Amy for Mrs. Earhart. From then on, she did not again directly mention her mother's coming to Rye for a visit.

When GP could tear himself away from his own projects and the business ventures he originated and managed for Amelia (which included airplane luggage, women's sports clothes, lounging pajamas and tailored suits, stationery called Amelia Earhart Time Savers, an endorsement of an automobile engine) the two arranged to meet occasionally wherever she was lecturing. Early in September, he was waiting at the airfield in Detroit when she flew in and crashed the autogiro on landing.

New York, September 17, 1931

Dear Mum,

. . . My giro spill was a freak accident. The landing gear gave way from a defect and I ground-looped
only. The rotors were smashed as usual with giros,
but there wasn't even a jar. GP fell over a wire running
to pick me up and as he limped up, I said, "It was
all my fault," meaning that he was hurt. The papers
got it I said the crack [up] was mine which
isn't accurate.

A

In the same letter and for the second time, Amelia sent word
to Muriel about the Morrissey house and the $2500 loan made
to her sister and brother-in-law. ". . . Tell Pidge I never received
anything further than the first notation of the mortgage
arrangements. I should like the certified copy accompanied with
notes which could be handled by a bank if desirable. These
can be just for record, but I should like them in that form . . ."

Muriel's failure to respond, as well as Mrs. Earhart's continued
resistance to leaving the Morrisseys even for a short time, resulted
in a coolness between Medford and Rye. There is no doubt that
Amelia loved both her mother and sister, but one wonders if she
ever understood either woman; if she, who could happily exist
by herself, ever acknowledged the need of most people *not* to be
solitary.

Over the years Amelia had voluntarily and aggressively chosen
to walk alone. Her mother and sister were too intelligent and
loving not to understand the ·desire for a career, but her
nonconformity was beyond the ability of either, even if they
envied her for it. Amelia's refusal to settle down and raise a
family, her willingness to leave home and husband for competition in a masculine field, or to break another record or keep a
lecture engagement, violated the social conventions by which
they lived. Amy had followed her husband until the divorce,

and was now happy to settle into the historical role of indispensable grandmother. Muriel, almost totally absorbed in her family, her church, and her teaching, was grateful to have her.

Both women loved Amelia, delighted in her rare visits, and relied on her for advice and financial aid as they would have relied on the man of the family. But the news stories they read about her and the questions they were asked about her and about themselves were alien to their world, and in hers they were strangers and ill at ease.

With money AE was impulsively generous on the one hand and coldly hardheaded on the other. It was rumored that her marriage to GP had been influenced in part by his unerring ability to raise financial backing for undertakings which interested him, and Amelia admitted after the wedding "...thus for me, can joyful luxuries like low-wing monoplanes be had." She considered her marriage "a reasonable and contented partnership" and would have hooted at any mention of Prince Charming.

The pair kept their funds scrupulously separate and divided all expenses exactly; anything left over was placed in a mutual savings fund. This was contrary to the proprieties in the belief of Amy Otis Earhart. As far as she was concerned, she was dependent, but in the old tradition she was also obligated to dispense charity: "Everything given to you was given for you to share with others." Someone had always shared with her and someone always would, while she in turn must share whatever she had with those who had not.

Fearing if anything fatal happened, her mother would give away everything left, Amelia made continued attempts to secure Amy's future and tried repeatedly to teach her the simplest kind of thrift — an undertaking which failed all around. Amy Earhart was often foolishly generous to the day of her death.

When Amelia was frustrated in her efforts, she wrote arrogantly to her mother, and made herself sound petty and unattractive.

Rye, [Fall of 1931]

Dear Mother,

I am enclosing a check for $33. This plus the $17 I sent last month makes $50. I am depositing the rest of the amount to your credit here. I am very much displeased at the use you have put what I hoped you would save. I am not working to help Albert, nor Pidge much as I care for her. If they had not had that money perhaps they would have found means to economize before.

I do not mean to be harsh, but I know the family failing about money. As for your paying board, such a thing is unthinkable as you have done all the house-keeping which more than compensates. I would not if I could, buy the bond. If there were any assurance that things were run on a businesslike basis, there might be some reason for helping.

It is true that I have a home and food but what I send you is what I myself earn and it does not come from GP. I feel the church gets some of what should go to living expenses and I have no wish to continue that to Pidge's loss...

When you send the pictures, send all and I'll return what aren't used.

Yr. doter

A.

The pictures were for Amelia's new book *The Fun of It*, which Harcourt, Brace was to publish the following year.

Spartanburg, South Carolina
[November 13, 1931]

Dear Mother,

Here I am in South Carolina. It is exactly, in weather, like California to date. I am touring around with a giro and plan to keep at it for a week or so before returning.

I have nothing until I am again at Rye for Uncle Thee. I believe then I can dig up some woollies [sic] and will ship them to you.

Let me know how Pidge and Albert progress...

If you want to reach me you can do so thru Nora at Rye.

A

In December Amelia scribbled a note with her mother's check saying she had just returned from a "strenuous southern trip," and as usual the two families spent the holidays apart.

After New Year of 1932, Amelia sounded more like herself when in her own special language she wrote to Amy.

Rye, [January 5, 1932]

Dear Mar,

Here is the keck as Dad used to say the Swedes said it.

I am glad the Chrizmoz things were OK. Tell Pidge I am sending her a birthdayer as soon as I get to town again. I have been so busy with my book I have not been out of the house much. However that is almost finished now. I'll send you proofs soon and also return the pictures none of which I could use.

Tootie Challiss was out the other day. She is just the same as she was. I hadn't seen her for five years I think. She has a temporary job and no plans...

Yrs.

A

Rye, [February 13, 1932]

Dear Mother,

I am very sorry to hear of your illness. I think it would have been better to let me know than let things get so bad. I am writing to Pidge to tell me who the doctor is and other information. Please feel I will see to hospital expenses. Don't worry about that end...I should prefer to pay the bills direct if you will have them forwarded here.

About Pidge. Why don't you suggest to her that Albert...go to Dr. Pecic and get a little information? Surely if Pidge can't manage things it is important for him to do so. Anyway I think he should share the mechanics of being a husband, as one [partner] should not bear the whole responsibility.

Please let me know how you get along.

A.E.

Popular psychology today might see a complex female triad distorted by a male intruder, but in the family climate then, Amelia's rancorous compulsions to provide for and withhold from her mother at the same time, and to offer unsolicited financial and contraceptive advice to her sister, reflected the contradictory quality of her own nature aggravated by her dissatisfaction with the person she had become at thirty-four. The belief that woman was created to serve man and bear children was totally unacceptable, and the unquestioning companionship and emotional support she had known with Amy she did not find with GP.

After the *Friendship* flight in 1928, she had existed in an aura of glory not of her making, and in her opinion one which was completely unjustified. She lived up to the public image GP had created and now promoted so diligently, not for herself or for the accumulation of wealth, but for the sake of aviation in general and aviation for women in particular. A sensitive, private woman, her face and name were known worldwide, and she was always under pressure. It never let up, not even when she and GP met at home together, because it was never her family who came to visit, but his sons; not often her friends, but fellow celebrities whom they knew jointly.

Since they had agreed not "to let the world see our private joys and disagreements," it is likely the first year of marriage was more difficult than Amelia had anticipated. She herself wrote later, at a time when she was to meet her husband somewhere, that she didn't know if it would be "more or less strenuous with him."

Inevitably these two strong-willed individuals clashed privately over many matters. One famous quarrel became a part of the legend. Putnam had arranged for the manufacture of some shoddy hats with Amelia's signature on the band. Costing about fifty cents apiece, they were to sell for three dollars. AE was horrified. She thought the hats dreadful and said selling them to children would be cheating. Eventually, and one assumes without grace, GP canceled the contract.

At the beginning of 1932, Amelia was not only exhausted from the fall lecture schedule, the autogiro trip, and work on her new manuscript, she was increasingly restless under the double confinement of work and marriage. Her mother and sister were absorbed in the Morrissey babies, and her husband had his film projects which kept him traveling between Hollywood and New York. Ahead for AE were only more lectures on old topics, more articles on old ideas, more of what she had been doing for the past four years.

This was another crisis of decision. She could rest on the legend or she could strike out alone. The endeavor would tax the limit of her strength, but if successful it would justify the glory and quiet her own suspicion that she was a fraud. She had been asked often enough when she was going to fly the Atlantic solo. Now seemed the time to attempt it.

THIRTEEN

"I Came from America" 1932

The Putnams were at breakfast one spring morning when Amelia asked over the buttermilk if George would mind her flying the Atlantic alone. For answer, he invited their friend Bernt Balchen to lunch to discuss the proposition. The Norwegian flyer had been with Roald Amundsen on the 1926 North Pole flight in a dirigible, and as pilot with the Richard E. Byrd expedition to the South Pole in 1929. Knowing Amelia and listening to her thoughtful appraisal of the problems involved, he assured her she was ready for the venture, and agreed to be her technical adviser.

To avoid publicity, Amelia chartered her red and gold Vega to Balchen, ostensibly for a South Pole flight he was planning with Lincoln Ellsworth. Balchen took it to Teterboro Airport in New Jersey and brought in Eddie Gorski, an expert Lockheed mechanic to recondition the plane AE had flown for the past three years. All the ailerons were replaced, a new engine and auxiliary fuel tanks were installed, and a drift indicator, two new compasses, and a directional gyrocompass were added to the instrument panel.

Preparing the plane in two months was one thing, preparing Amelia was another. Technically she was honed keen, having over a thousand flying hours in weather of all kinds to her credit, but she needed practice in navigating on instruments, as well as added weather training with Dr. Kimball. She insisted, therefore, on total secrecy concerning the flight, so she could go about as usual without having to deal with reporters. She had more work to do on her new book, her spring lecture schedule to keep, and as usual the family was on her mind.

> Rye, [April 5, 1932]
>
> Dear Mother,
>   Xcuse paper. I am writing hastily and have none other handy...Please tell Pidge that her Easter is coming. Nora has gone to South America and I cannot get things done as well as of yore without her. She will be back I expect or I shall have to have someone in her stead as I cannot keep up with mail alone...
>   Have I ever sent you pix of the house? Now that spring is coming, I'd like you to see it as the garden grows. I forget whether you have had a look or not.
>   I haven't been paying the scrub woming. I think she ought to come anyway, so don't protest too loudly at her ministrations.
>
>   Love
>   A.E.

When Mrs. Earhart remained steadfastly with Muriel in Medford, Amelia went as she could to visit, but she said no word of her plans for the transatlantic flight.

Bernt Balchen and Eddie Gorski were to fly the Vega to Harbour Grace, Newfoundland, so Amelia would be rested for the long flight alone, and by May 18 everything was ready to go. A low-pressure area with heavy clouds and rain lingered in the northeastern Atlantic, however, and there was nothing to do but wait for better weather.

On Friday May 20, Amelia arrived at the Teterboro Airport late in the morning, resigned to a chat with the men and a bit of practice flying. At noon George telephoned from Dr. Kimball's office. The weather between New York and Harbour Grace was "perfect."

Amelia gave no thought to lunch. She drove to Rye, changed into jodhpurs and windbreaker, stopped a minute to "soak up the beauty of the pink and white dogwood blossom outside the bedroom window," and after telling the housekeeper not to prepare dinner that evening raced back to Teterboro. Later she wrote, "My tanks were filled under the guidance of Major Edwin Aldrin..." In 1969, his son, Colonel Edwin E. Aldrin, Jr., would be the second man to step on the moon. That day, however, George was already at the airport to see Amelia off. He gave her a twenty-dollar bill and asked her to telephone him as soon as the plane landed.

With AE lying on the floor of the fuselage behind an extra fuel tank, Gorski beside her, and Balchen at the controls, the red and gold Vega took off to the north. Although GP said later that because he had made a "general nuisance of himself by phoning around the newspaper offices" during the 1928 flight, this time he had not. Still, somehow word was leaked that in Newfoundland Amelia Earhart was "poised for an attempt to be the first woman to make a solo flight across the Atlantic."

On Friday evening at Harbour Grace, after a nap and further weather information from GP by telegraph, Amelia listened to last-minute instructions from Bernt Balchen. Dressed in her baggy flying suit with large button-down pockets over each knee, she looked at him with "a small lonely smile" and asked if he thought she could make it. "You bet," he told her.

In a "lingering sunset" at 7:12 P.M., she was airborne and alone, and there followed more than 15 hours of fighting ice on the wings and fearing flames from a broken weld on the manifold of the motor. The altimeter failed, and she "was considerably buffeted about and with difficulty" held her course. She was forced to fly just above the waves to avoid ice, and she plowed "through the 'soup' and [didn't] look out of the cockpit again until the morning came." With her exhaust manifold vibrating and her reserve fuel tank gauge leaking, she decided to abandon the try for France and come down wherever she saw land.

She never later commented at length on her emotional reactions, being as in the past constitutionally unwilling or unable to show her deepest feelings, but she must have known terror as she contemplated death and decided she would rather "drown than burn"; and she must have panicked when she spun out at 3000 feet and ended at "— well, something above the water." On June 21, in her speech to the National Geographic Society, she remarked, "Probably if I had been able to see what was happening on the outside during the night I would have had heart failure then and there; but, as I could not see, I carried on."

Fortunately Ireland was just ahead beneath the clouds, and AE followed a railroad to a long sloping meadow near Londonderry, where she "frightened all the cows in the county," as she landed. It was Saturday afternoon, May 21, the fifth anniversary of Colonel Charles A. Lindbergh's arrival in France. In 15 hours and 39 minutes, Amelia Earhart had flown 2026 miles to prove herself his equal, and established three records no human being could ever break. She was the first woman to fly the Atlantic, the first to fly it solo, and the first person ever to fly it twice.

Weariness held her in the cockpit for a few minutes after she stopped rolling down that long sloping meadow in Ireland, and then she said aloud, "I've done it," and put away forever the idea of herself as a fraudulent heroine.

A farmer came to the plane to stare in at her.

Amelia grinned. "Hi! I've come from America."

"Have you now," Farmer Gallagher exclaimed.

Eventually he summoned a constable to protect the plane from a small crowd of curious citizens, and in a borrowed car drove Amelia six miles along the road to a neighbor who had a telephone. When she got through to George in New York and told him where she was, he asked if she wanted him to come over, and she told him she knew he was busy, she would wait forty-eight hours and see what happened. Meantime would he phone her mother and sister and break the news to them, please?

Then Farmer Gallagher drove her back to his house, where

she had a meal and slept the rest of the afternoon and all night.

On Sunday in Londonderry, when she arrived at the Associated Press office, there were already cables and messages. One from the Lindberghs, who were in deep mourning for their murdered son: WE DO CONGRATULATE YOU STOP YOUR FLIGHT IS A SPLENDID SUCCESS. And one from Ruth Nichols, who had been preparing to make the same flight: YOU BEAT ME TO IT FOR THE SECOND TIME BUT IT WAS A SPLENDID JOB...Phil Cooper, owner of a dry cleaning establishment used by the Putnams, cabled, KNEW YOU WOULD DO IT STOP I NEVER LOSE A CUSTOMER. Lady Astor offered to "lend her a night-gown," Amy and Muriel sent love and congratulations, President Herbert Hoover complimented "the capacity of women to match the skill of men," and the Marquess of Londonderry delivered a message of pleasure from King George and Queen Mary on her success.

People kept crowding around to peer at her and to touch her, questions came at her from all sides, more messages were handed to her, and after some time Amelia went to seek a telephone. When she reached George in New York, she asked him to catch the next ship for Europe.

Three days later, just before he sailed for Cherbourg, GP wrote Amy a letter beginning, "Dear Mrs. Earhart." He promised to take letters to Amelia in France, and said they were coming back on a slow boat so AE could rest. He asked if Amy and Muriel would like to come to New York to meet him and Amelia on their return. His secretary would arrange accommodations, but of course it would be "hectic" and perhaps they would "prefer to keep out of things and come later to visit at Rye." That chore disposed of, he boarded the SS *Olympic*, eager to reach France and take charge of his wife.

Paramount News had flown Amelia to London, where she stayed at the American Embassy with Ambassador Andrew W. Mellon and his family. She was given the Certificate of Honorary Membership of the British Guild of Airpilots and Navigators, only the second non-British pilot to receive the honor. She attended many luncheons and dinners, and met with the Prince of Wales, who in the year of her disappearance and death would become king and then abdicate. Henry and Gordon Selfridge arranged for her gold and red monoplane to be shipped from Ireland and hung inside their store on Oxford Street before it was sent home. At a luncheon of the British Institute of Journalists, the newsmen gave Amelia an ovation, and she said, "The nicest thing that has happened to me is having all these men stand and sing 'For She's a Jolly Good Fellow.' "

On June 2, she wrote to Amy from Lady Astor's house at 4 St. James's Square, Kensington, S.W.1.

> Dear Mother,
> I am awaiting Lady Astor's return so snatch a moment to drop you a line. G.B. Shaw is being towed in to meet me or I him. I leave on a yacht for Cherbourg this afternoon, meeting G.P.P. tomorrow morning. Thence to Paris. I thought I couldn't face coming home alone.
> I was glad to get your and Pidge's cables. I'll have some surprises for you when I return which will probably be about June 10.
> L.O.L.
> A.

In the envelope with this letter was a clipping from an unidentified newspaper, reporting that George Bernard Shaw told Amelia Earhart "just what I thought of her, and you had better ask her about it." Informed that Miss Earhart was at sea on her way to France, the playwright chuckled and said, "That's just as well."

After a private reunion aboard the yacht *Evadne*, Amelia and her husband went by train to Paris, where the pace for the next several days increased cruelly. She was presented with the Cross of the Legion of Honor, attended the Air Races, and laid wreaths at the Tomb of the Unknown Soldier and the monument to the Lafayette Escadrille. Crowds gathered to get close, to catch her eye, to pat her cheek or touch her hand or arm or shoulder or her hair, to pull and tug at her clothing as if to tear it off, until she shrank away. She was now and would always be on public display, like it or not.

From Paris the couple went to Rome for private meetings with Mussolini and the Pope, and back to Paris, only to journey a few days later to Brussels for luncheon with the Belgian King and Queen, followed by the presentation of the Cross of Chevalier of the Order of Leopold. Afterward Amelia and George visited Auguste Piccard, and GP suggested the possibility of a stratospheric balloon flight for Amelia with the Belgian pioneer. Nothing ever came of the idea, although Dr. Piccard later visited the Putnams at Rye, and dined there one evening with the Lindberghs.

On June 15, after a civic reception in Le Havre, the Putnams sailed on the *Ile de France*. Three airplanes escorted the liner to sea and dropped flowers on the deck as France's farewell to Amelia Earhart. She had been away from home for less than a month, and she had not seen her mother and sister for longer than that; but they had taken George's hint and did not meet the ship when it docked in New York.

FOURTEEN

Honors
and Medals
1932-1933

In Washington on June 21, a month after the solo flight, Amelia in a long white low-necked gown, with George at her side, was guest of honor at a formal White House dinner with President and Mrs. Herbert Hoover. Afterward the assemblage adjourned to Constitution Hall, national auditorium of the Daughters of the American Revolution, where 10,000 requests had been received for the 3800 seats available.

Among others on the platform were the Chief Justice of the United States Supreme Court and Mrs. Hughes, and in the audience were cabinet members, senators and congressmen, ambassadors and ministers from twenty-two countries, military officers, scientists, men of letters, and other distinguished members of the National Geographic Society. The United States Marine Band played "Hail to the Chief" as President Hoover entered with Amelia on his arm.

At exactly nine o'clock, over its total network of thirty-eight radio stations, the National Broadcasting Company relayed the formalities coast to coast across the nation. Dr. Gilbert Grosvenor, President of the National Geographic Society, mentioned in his introduction that not only was Amelia Earhart the first woman to cross the Atlantic by air, the first to cross it alone, and the only person in the world to cross it twice, she was the first woman to be awarded the Society's Special Gold Medal, which only eight pilots had received previously.

President Hoover spoke of Amelia's ability and achievements as "in spirit with the great pioneering women to whom every generation of Americans has looked up, with admiration for their firmness of will, their strength of character, and their cheerful spirit of comradeship in the work of the world...Mrs. Putnam has made all mankind her debtor by her demonstration of new possibilities of the human spirit and the human will in overcoming barriers of space and restrictions of Nature on the radius of human activity..."

In accepting the medal, Amelia disclaimed the honor as "too great" for her exploit, later saying that her flight had "added nothing to aviation." She discounted exaggerations in the newspapers — she had *not* landed "within six feet of a hedge of trees," and she did have more than one gallon of gasoline left because she had to pay Irish taxes on one hundred gallons. Furthermore, she did not kill a cow in landing "unless one died of fright." She described flying on instruments as a "significant step in aviation," and she paid tribute to Bernt Balchen as her adviser, because in her opinion "any expedition owes 60 per cent of its success to the preparation beforehand." She hoped that transatlantic travel would become commonplace, and "that the flight has meant something to women in aviation. If it has, I shall feel it was justified; but I can't claim anything else..."

As Mrs. Hoover later remarked, "...If a girl was to fly across the Atlantic alone and so, in a sense, represent America before the world, how nice it is that [she] was such a person as Miss Earhart. She is poised, well bred, lovely to look at, and so intelligent and sincere." Amelia's sincerity came through to everyone who heard her, including the Congress of the United States, which on the following day received her at the Capitol in joint session and signified its intention to award her the Distinguished Flying Cross, the first woman to receive the honor.

Mrs. Hoover might also have noted that Amelia was full of energy, not only able to withstand the rigors of a long night flight with only a can of tomato juice to nourish her, but to speak much as she had in Washington night after night and many times in the morning or afternoon too, on lecture schedules that would have worn out anyone of lesser stamina.

Following the National Geographic Society's ceremonies, Amelia was honored several times in New York, and on June 29 flew to Boston for an official civic reception. Amy and Muriel met her at the airport, but there was little time for family talk. They rode several cars behind Amelia in the procession, and spent the afternoon at the hotel, watching as she greeted civic and state dignitaries. In the evening they attended the banquet in her honor, and of course George was there. The following day Amelia flew her husband to California, where he had film business. They stayed at the Ambassador Hotel.

> Los Angeles, [July 5, 1932]
>
> Dear Mother,
>   Here we are. Enclosed is a check for 100 berries.
>   It was nice seeing you even in the rush. Toot and Katch [Lucy and Katherine Challiss] are both at Rye holding the house down while we are here. I want you to come when I return in August.
>   Cheerio for now,
>   A.

> Rye, [July 20, 1932]
>
> Dear Mrs. Eho,
>   I've sent some presents mostly usefuls — you will see. I didn't send you all I intended because I have some interesting plans for later...
>   I didn't mean to give you a session with the dentist as a Xmas gift but it may be necessary to look at [it] so for a while.
>   Please see Pidge doesn't pull an "Aunty" and buy the children something with her birthday check. I sent it specifically for dark gloves hat and alterations on

skirt and nothing else. She ought to look swell in the suit if she'll get decent accessories...

A

Will write later.

In the same envelope as this letter was an undated note:

Dear Mother
    Am on my way to Detroit. Then to Calif. if plans work out.

A.

On July 28 Amelia returned to Los Angeles by automobile from Taft, California, where faulty gasoline pressure had forced her down on her flight from New York. The next day, Vice President Charles Curtis presented her with the actual Distinguished Flying Cross and Congressional Citation at a ceremony preceding his dedication of the new State building. On Sunday July 31, he opened the 1932 Summer Olympic Games.

Amelia attended the games, and at some point, an enterprising Associated Press photographer got her to pose in the company of the Hawaiian swimmer Duke Kahanamoku, Gold Medal winner of 1912 and 1920; the great Finnish runner Paavo Nurmi, winner in 1920 and 1924; Arthur Jonath, a German sprinter; and movie actor Douglas Fairbanks, senior, who with his wife Mary Pickford was a good friend. Gold Medal winners of 1932 who must have pleased Amelia were the great Mildred "Babe" Didrikson in the 80-meter hurdles and javelin throw, Helene Madison in the 100-meter and 400-meter freestyle swiming races, and Georgia Coleman in the springboard diving competition.

Los Angeles, August 5, 1932

Dear Mother,
    I am enclosing a check for $100, as usual...

I saw Cousin Rilla [Challiss] the other evening. . .and had a fleeting glance at Cousin Jim, who was leaving for the East (by train of course). Tootie is the only aviation fan in the family. She came with me by air, as you may have seen in the news dispatches. . .

I have enjoyed the Olympic Games immensely. Conditions are ideal and you know what a track fan I have always been.

I'll write you later if anything turns up.

Sincerely yours,
Yr. doter

On August 24 Amelia turned her plane east and set the women's transcontinental speed record by flying nonstop from Los Angeles to Newark in 19 hours and 5 minutes; eleven months later she would break it.

New York, Labor Day
[September 6, 1932]

Dear Maw,

Harye? I hope you have had a nice summer. As you know I have been west mostly and only yesterday returned from the Air Races at Cleveland.

What are your plans? Are you going to stay in Miggleshead for the autumn? I know that is a life saver for Pidge to have you keeping David, and I think she would have been downed otherwise.

This is the situation with me. I am to be home except for little jaunts until the latter part of October. Then I start on a lecture program which will carry me through Nov. and the first part of Dec. I haven't yet got the final itinery [sic] but there might be a chance of your going along part of the way if you would like to. I shall fly or drive as I wont travel on trains. It might be just one hotel after another. I'll let you know what the schedule looks like later. The whole idea may be a pipe dream.

Otherwise I wanted you down here at Rye for a week

this month or next. Lemme know what you'd like. You ain't never seen the place.

L.o.L.

A.

Rye, September 18, 1932

Dear Maw,

I am sorry not to have been able to answer your plea for a lil cash sooner but I have been so very busy that I couldn't get around to family affairs. Here is half of what you wanted. I thought if I sent the whole you would spend it on someone else and so have nothing left for yourself by the first of next month...

I have not worked out details of how you and I can tour. If you come back to Mudford from Mubblehead during this month, let me know. Possibly it would be well for you to come down to Rye for a day or two and work out details.

I sent Pidge a box of castoffs which will be too large for David but probably can be reduced to fit him. I wish she were smaller — so many of my things could be used.

I sent you a Geographic with an article on the presentation of the medal.

LOL

A

Rye, October 4, 1932

Dear Mother,

I don't know what I said to give you the impression that I was taking Tootie with me on my tour. She is going to be here and I think would be far more useful running the house than in the car with me. The original plan I outlined is still under consideration. I'll let you know about it...

The lovely silver sherbert [sic] cups came sometime ago and I was under the impression I had thanked you for them before. They finish out my set very well. Six of anything is usually inadequate for our service as you will see when you come down.

Keep me informed what happens in Medford.

Sincerely,

A

New York, [November 4, 1932]

Dear Mother,

I just returned from Chicago and points west where I have had one of the first of my lectures. Everything went well. I flew and trained when necessary and did not attempt to go so far by car.

I shall be here ten days and then start out in New England. GP is going with me to the most northern points as I do not like the territory very well as you know and need moral support. I am enclosing my ininery [sic] so you may keep track of my whereabouts, there may be some changes but not many.

I don't know what to say about your accompanying. I thought from one crack you made that you didn't really care to go. You said maybe it was just as well that you didn't go so there could be no chance of your disgracing me or words to that effect. However there may be ways yet if you want to for a few days, and I'll try to work something out.

I could hardly believe my eyes when you suggested that you might like to take the children to California. Is that figurative or did you mean it? I thought you never would care to see that land again. What would M think of letting the youngsters go anywhere?

I am glad the box suited. The nightie is for you and the tan robe. I'll send slips to match when I get down town.

A

Rye, December 24, 1932

Dear Mother,

As usual I got caught and didn't send my Xmas box in time to reach Mudford for the holiday. However it will come.

I am glad you didn't get me anything. You know I am not much on holidays for themselves. I only remember the family except with cards...

I have been away so much that your check was delayed. I am home now for a few weeks and then start west for a few lectures on the coast. I have sold my plane to the Franklin Institute in Phil. for their aviation room as a permanent exhibit. I shall have to get another one for my use soon and it will probably be another of the same kind.

I had a very interesting time at Thiel [Thiel College, Greenville, Pennsylvania]. I met several people who were in Dad's class and others who knew him. I found his record for scholarship, ie., age of graduation, has never been equalled. He was fourteen when he entered college and only eighteen when he got his degree. The crowd at the convocation was the greatest ever assembled and a number were turned away.

Everyone remembered Dad as so handsome and bright. His nickname was "Kid." I didn't know that slang was popular then. "Kid Earhart" now sounds like a prize fighter. His best friend and class mate introduced me, a nice old codger who was once president of the college and now lives in N.J. He said he saw [Dad] last in Phila. when he came there some years ago and bunked in his rooms. I don't know whether this was before or after you were married.

I stayed all night and then drove to Toronto in a sleet storm. I had a nice time there and saw Mildred Trant Robertson and Mrs. Holland who has been ill several years but is getting along now. Toronto has changed a lot, but I could recognize some haunts. Miss McDonald was at my lecture and asked to be remembered to Pidge. St. Mags [St. Margaret's College] closed the year after Muriel was there. The way to reach her is thru the University Women's Club if Pidge wishes to write.

Among other things I sent you a lil dress. I am sure the neck will be too small for you so have the tailor cut it down and *bind* it, otherwise it will tear. Whatever he does won't show as the tie comes over.

Well as I started out to say Murry Xmas.

[Unsigned]

Rye, January 27, 1933

Dear Mother,

Your interpretation of the hang-dog picture is not at all correct. I feared to look too joyful on the occasion [of the presentation of] the Roumanian medal, — so looked too sad. As a matter of fact, I am quite able to stand and weigh now as much as I ever have in my life. I have been drinking cream and gained ten pounds — so that's that.

I am just rushing to catch the Century [Limited] over by Tarrytown for Chicago. I intended to fly but Western storms coming in prevented. As I am due in Portland, Oregon on the first, I have to start...

I won't have time to sign this letter, so I am asking Mrs. Weber to sign it and send it on.

Your doter —
Amelia

Rye, [February 13, 1933]

Dear Mother,

I am just back from California — three days there — and a lecture tour. These are the last of the scheduled lectures. They were much more intensive than I had planned because the management [G.P.] kept trying to squeeze in more, and in these times I thought I might as well do as much and get as much as I could. Well, anyway they are over now.

I am going to Chicago the end of this week for a wedding. I loathe the formal kind and have never attended any since Pidge got me inside a church for hers. (I don't mean only church weddings are awful, of course.)

I had a grand time flying out to Seattle via the Northern route. So much of the territory we covered.

Do you remember Cheallis [Chehalis, Washington]? The country is lovely from the air. The snow is fifty feet deep and the mountains are covered into Calif.

Enclosed is a check. Please don't give it all away if the giving means fostering dependence and lack of responsibility.

Yr. doter

A

New York, [March 6, 1933]

Dear Maw,

I am glad you liked the picture. I'll send more from time to time as new ones are taken. If they don't make you sick — so many...

I am glad you told me of Uncle Clarence's death. I didn't know. It was best that it happened, I think.

Yr. doter

A

A lil package is on the way. Many happies on the seventh.

The White House, April 20, 1933

Dear Mother,

GP and I are staying here tonight. You may hear of our visit officially but this is a personal note.

I hope Pidge finally received the papers she wished. I left them here to be sent and then found that they had been held up for a notary's signature.

I had sent you some few weeks ago a couple of bottles of tooth wash. Nusol [?] it is called and it is the only scientific solvent on the market. My dentist says it is the best he knows and none of the usual ones do any good whatsoever.

I sent Pidge a package the other day. I hope "it" fits.

Cheerio

A

P. S. I thot the pictures good. The pink ones are attractive themselves but like you I don't care for the finish. You need not tell the photographers so, however. I did notice a couple of things. That display of garter on sister's fat knee [young Amy Morrissey]. Do please have Pidge let the children wear sox so they don't look like bumpkins. And why the silly hair ribbon? I'll buy em 6 pairs of sox each if she will use them.

A

If writing from the White House of socks and hair ribbons and toothwash seems incongruous, it was not out of character but confirmation that in her own mind Amelia largely separated her mother and sister from her public life, even as they did their best to stand clear of the legend — the legend who was known all over the world, who mingled comfortably with the famous and visited at the White House yet retained a strong interest in family events and trivia.

George Putnam had called the Hoover White House "pathetically dedicated to gloom," but the energetic Roosevelts drastically changed the atmosphere. Amelia frequently stayed unofficially with the First Family, and once, unable to appear at meals because of her own schedule, was misquoted when asked how she liked it there. "I haven't eaten enough to know," she answered, which appeared in print as "I never seem to get enough to eat there." Amelia wired apologies to Mrs. Roosevelt and later wrote, "I only hope some day I can laugh . . . at the preposterous 'starvation interview' the press has had me give concerning my stay at the White House. . . I am humiliated that any incident should have occurred to mar what to me was so delightful an interlude." Mrs. Roosevelt responded affectionately that she hoped Amelia would visit again, and in a postscript added, "I shall give you a key to the icebox next time."

When in May Mrs. Earhart finally came to visit Amelia at Rye, she possibly was given the upstairs guest bedroom with the murals of tropical fish and marine growth on the walls. At the lively dinner table she turned up her hearing aid and nodded and smiled as if she had caught all the conversation among the family and guests, always guests, some famous and some obscure. The food was sometimes prepared by her energetic and talkative son-in-law, but more often by the cook-housekeeper whose husband was butler-chauffeur as needed, and only occasionally by Amelia. While her daughter was busy in the office under the stairs where the walls were covered with clippings and photos, she probably wrote letters or took a turn in the kitchen for one of her famous chocolate puddings. She had little unhurried time with Amelia, who never appeared to rush but never paused long anywhere.

Rye, May 30, 1933

Dear Mother,

I have sent you several packages the contents of which are to be allotted as follows: everything for you which isn't obviously for Albert...I owe you some more clothing, ie. the jacket to your linen, a scarf for your yellow silk, some light hose to wear with white shoes. Also some mittens...

I have been busy since you left. You would not know the place. Tootie comes in the next week but GPP and I may not be here as we rather plan to go to Chicago for a while.

Ask Pidge if she needs any pictures for her house. I am cleaning out some we can't use here, illustrations for books etc. and I will send her several if she would like.

yr doter
A.E.

However they may have differed, whatever they may have said or done at one time or another, the difference in life styles was only superficial, and the deep feeling Amelia had for her mother and sister was strong and always would be, no matter how many times it was strained. As it was again, shortly after Amy returned to Medford.

FIFTEEN

Family Relations 1933-1934

People today cannot imagine how radio broadcasts interested and amused and instructed nearly everyone in the early 1930s. At a time when Walter Damrosch conducted the "Music Appreciation Hour" and Hendrik Willem van Loon taught "A Class in History," when Nobel Prize winner Arthur H. Compton lectured on "Cosmic Rays" and First Lady Eleanor Roosevelt discussed "The Woman as Wage Earner," all in one day's programming, it was inevitable for Amelia Earhart to broadcast in the interest of aviation. On February 24, 1933, she participated in a sketch called "The Inside Story" with Edwin C. Hill, and on May 26, she talked "from a plane with eight different points in New York," presumably from eight different locations above the city.

In addition to radio and her other pursuits, Amelia was invited to and often appeared at social and charitable functions not in her honor. Late in May such an event was the impressive ball given in New York for Mrs. Franklin D. Roosevelt for the benefit of lunchrooms and restrooms she had established for unemployed women seeking positions in the business district; these were located at 22 East 38th Street and at the Trade Unions Building at 247 Lexington Avenue. Among members of high society who attended were Hearsts, Astors, and Vanderbilts. Numerous luminaries of opera and stage gave of their talents, and the affair was a "spectacle of military and naval pageantry."

Amelia and George were present, but surely in the back of her mind was the disturbing letter she had had from Amy. To the logical Amelia, it was unthinkable to skip payment on a bill for any reason, and borrowing money for a treat was simply not done; but that was how Muriel managed. She had little patience with what she considered Pidge's inability to handle either money or her husband, and less for imposing on Mrs. Earhart, who was now in her midsixties, overworked and underappreciated, and now expected to assume total responsibility for David, who was four, and young Amy, who was three.

The new storm arose over summer plans for Mrs. Earhart.

Rye, [June 8, 1933]

Dear Mother,

I wired you from Cleveland where I had flown in a test hop. I did not want you to arrange to go to some Maine dump that none of us knew anything about when there are so many places that are available and better situated.

In the first place you are not to have both children. If you have David part of the time I cannot object but two is out of the question and I will not permit under any circumstances. You are not the kind of woman who has no other interest but brats and I do not see the necessity of your being a drudge and nurse maid...

Do you remember Elise Owen? She and her mother are taking in guests this summer in their old house at Stonington, Ct. I have been there and know it is a grand place...

If you can't go to Marblehead why not try this place? I probably could stake you [to] a large room with fireplace etc and three squares a day if you could get along with thirtyfive bucks a month. On the other hand, I think it would be better to pay a little more and go to Marblehead than a new place. Let me know your reactions immediately.

A

Rye, [June 24, 1933]

Dear Mother,

I am sorry I cannot change about your taking two children at one time. One at a time is a different story...

I do not like to be arbitrary but I do not see any other way of doing things. Anyway I think Pidge doesn't want to have both away. You didn't when you had two small brats and you didn't have the necessity of teaching DAD responsibility for them, either.

Yes, we received the honey and thank you muchly.

yr. doter

A

Rye [undated]

Dear Mrs. Eho,

You did not answer about the Owens' establishment in Stonington. In the meantime I hope you have settled on a Marblehead joint. However, I want your solemn word that you will not try to have two infants with you. I shall be compelled to withhold the monthly check if you do any such funny bizness. It is bad for you and for them too, and as I have pointed out for the Morrisseys. *It is absolutely out!!!*

...We just returned from the Fair in Chicago. We flew out and took June Put [GP's son] and needless to say we covered the whole show.

A

Among several obvious conflicts in the complex nature of Amelia Earhart was the desire to be loved and the need to dominate, common urges in everyone. The first made Amelia generous with gifts and money and attentions to her mother, from arranging for her future security to advice on dental hygiene. The second made her assume authority over her mother and sister to which she was not entitled. Beyond offering interested and helpful suggestions and opinions, it was really not her responsibility to say where and with whom her mother would spend the summer.

How greatly Muriel and Albert relied on Amy to help run the house and raise the Morrissey children was according to their need and Amy's willingness to serve. Amelia could only state her opinions, but since the household ran partly on funds she supplied, she believed she had a right as a concerned and caring daughter and silent financial participant in the family situation to determine what was best for all of them. It is plain, in this instance however, that Amelia's dismay was occasioned by more than the question of Amy's summer vacation, although it had nothing to do with her love. Its roots were in the deep and silent struggle between the sisters for their mother's attention. None of the three was aware of, and each would have vehemently denied its very existence. Nevertheless, Amelia's waspish letters to her mother and letters from Muriel to Amy which ignore Amelia's existence in favor of her own concerns are evidence that it underlay the triangular family pattern. In the deepest sense of all, the essential conflict was between Amelia and little Millie Earhart, who stood in the shadow of the legendary AE, with none of the three being quite sure who the other two were.

Putting down her private agitation in favor of her professional obligations, Amelia now concentrated on preparation for the Bendix transcontinental air derby in which she and Ruth Nichols were the sole female entrants. They would compete for a special women's prize of $2500, while the four male pilots would divide $9000 among them, with a $1000 bonus to the winner if he broke the present westward record of 12 hours and 39 minutes.

Amelia took off from Newark on July 1, made an overnight stop at Wichita, and came in third of all competitors at the Los Angeles Municipal Airport. Her red Lockheed Vega flew over at top speed, and she landed far down the field. When she taxied back to the reviewing stand, a crowd of 30,000 stood to cheer her. Ruth Nichols arrived the following day, and Amelia on her return to Newark in 17 hours and 7½ minutes broke her own record established a year ago. The two women, friends and neighbors at Rye, would continue to be rivals in establishing and breaking records as they had been since 1922.

Amelia and George were now deeply involved in setting up their own airline with Paul Collins, who had left TAT. A subsidiary of the Boston and Maine Railroad, the airline would operate five schedules in each direction daily between Boston and Portland, Maine, and two daily between Boston and Bangor. This meant Amelia went frequently to Boston on business, but she rarely had time even to telephone Medford.

Rye, [July 13, 1933]

Dear Mother,

This is a used sheet but none other seems available.

Enclosed is your sheck. I am sending it promply as I may have to go to Europe with GPP in a week or so and I want to get all obligations cleared before then...It is a business trip and I don't look forward to a stuffy ride over for a week there and a stuffy one back. I should not mind if I were staying to see something.

For my birthday, do not get anythink. We plan to close the house this winter as I am to lecture again and it looks as if there were several trips in the offing. It is very expensive keeping this place going and living around at the same time. However we haven't worked out plans definitely yet. So — if we don't go and don't give up the house, I'd like some steel knives, I think or small butter dishes (individual). I'll let you know when I know...

I hope you are getting some cool weather. Mayhap I'll be up that way some time next week. Don't tell.

A

In addition to business, the Putnams had celebrated guests visiting at Rye. James Mollison, a noted British pilot, and his wife Amy Johnson Mollison, a well-known pilot in her own right, had crash-landed in a marsh near Stratford, Connecticut, at the end of his second westbound transatlantic crossing. The previous year he had made the first westbound solo in a De Havilland Puss Moth from Portmarnock, Ireland, to Pennfield, New Brunswick. Amelia had gone to see the couple in the hospital where they were recovering from minor injuries, and invited them to Rye for the remainder of their convalescence.

Mrs. Earhart spent July and August at Marblehead and if she had one or both children with her, Amelia was too preoccupied to mention it when she wrote to her mother.

Rye, [September 16, 1933]

Dear Mother,

I am sorry not to have sent your check before. So many more things than usual have conspired to keep me busy however, that I forgot. GP went to Paris in my stead. I did not want to go on just a business trip so begged off the last few days. The airline has taken a lot of time, so much so that I have been unable to call Pidge, or see you, on my hasty visits to Boston...

I am sending this to Muriel's, as I am not sure whether you are still in Marblehead...Do you want to stay in Marblehead anyway until the autumn is over? I should think that would be a good idea for, after all the rain we have had we should have a beautiful Indian summer. About plans later I have some ideas which I will let you know soon...

I am off on a lecture tour about October first. Let me know your immediate wishes as there might be time for you to come here for a week before I go. Mrs. Putman (can't spell my own name) is here but goes to Noank tomorrow.

Tootie just telephoned she has a new job which will take her travelling. She has helped me a lot as I have no regular secretary.

Probably GP and I will live in NY this winter. I don't like the idea but I shall be away so much that it seems extravagant to keep up the house. But I think the country is much better for us, and we haven't decided yet. We might rent the place if we could and keep the present servants. It is hard to get such good ones.

A

Amelia drove Amy to Chicago in late September. They spent a few days visiting the Exposition and shopping, and then Amelia left her mother at the Shedds' for a visit. She herself went on to keep the first of twenty-three speaking engagements in twenty-five days.

Sioux City, Iowa
[October 7, 1933]

Dear Mother,

I hope you got some food after I left you before you became too "hollow." I worried about your missing lunch. However I hope the nice hat and shoon made up for the lack of food. Did Fields [Marshall Field, department store] send everything out as promised?

I drove here all the way and arrived about four thirty a.m. It was a gorgeous night and I thought I'd rather sleep for a few hours after I reached Sioux City than to get up at an early hour and drive from somewhere along the way to arrive for luncheon. The roads have certainly improved from the days when you and I knew them. They are elegant now and almost as well marked as [in] California.

I sent your jacket back today. I thought I had all your things out when I repacked the car. I believe you have plenty without it, even so.

I am off to Wayne Nebraska tomorrow, then Mason City, then Minneapolis. I have to shoot down to Fort Leavenworth from there but I may come through

Chicago en route. If so I'll call to see if you're about. If I don't come by, I'll let you know anyway. By the way I just found another itinerary which you may keep.

Don't be afraid to spend money. Whatever you need to do in reason is OK. I missed a ten plunk bill after I left you and only hope I gave it to you rather than lost it.

A

Atchison, Kansas
[October 15, 1933]

Dear Mrs. Eho,

Will you vote for Challiss for Congress? This is some of the campaign paper that Cousin Jim used when he was going to run and it is all I can find hereabout. I am staying with the Challisses as you can guess while I lecture at Fort Leavenworth and Maryville, instead of Omaha. I have seen Mary and Theodore [Uncle Thee] and Mrs. Beitzel and Mrs. Drury. Tomorrow I must see Mrs. Fox and Nellie Webb is going to interview me for the Globe. Everyone is very cordial and it seems that "Millie has not changed at all" — heaven help her.

When I was at Emporia, day before yesterday, Barbara came up to me and said she had taken care of me as a little girl. I faintly remembered her and asked her name. She said Mrs. Pete Brown. She has had five girls and four boys or vice versa and I said I'd tell you I saw her. She'd burst if you dropped her a note. Then there I also saw several people whose names were Altmen who said they were cousins of Dad's. I never heard of them but said I'd take their word for the relationship. I really have been having a sort of old home week. Everyone asks about you. Lissa Campbell is writing you and you will probably hear from several others.

I picked up my shoes at the Fort today. Thenkee. I didn't know what had happened to them.

About your staying at the Shedds. I expect to be terribly busy in Chicago with outside appointments so will not have much time for seeing anyone. However, if you want to stay until the twentieth, I could put you on the train back and maybe pay my respects to the Shedds. I'll call when I get there to see what you have done. Don't hesitate to cash the check for what you need in the meantime. If you run short ask Mr. S. to advance you some and I will repay him when I arrive. I hope you have liked the fair.

I'll write you again soon. Cousin Rilla asks that you come here and pay her a lil visit while in the territory.

A.

The article that Nellie Webb wrote made headlines: AMELIA EARHART IS GUEST HERE/ FAMOUS AVIATRIX VISITS HER MAIDEN CITY/ ON WESTERN SPEAKING TRIP/ GLOBE REPORTER INTERVIEWS FLIER AT J. M. CHALLISS HOME. Not that these were different from other headlines at other times in other newspapers, big city or small town, it made no difference: Amelia was news. As Nellie Webb wrote in the Atchison *Globe,* her "name since she was the first woman to make a solo flight across the Atlantic, has been written in electric lights in the world's history..."

Amelia sent the clipping to Amy who was still in Chicago.

Des Moines, Iowa
[October 19, 1933]

Here's the Globe's idea of yr doter. Cousin Rilla says its ok but the luxurious divan which is her old sofa.

Many people have called me here, none I really knew well.

I saw Annie Cain yesterday and drove here after speaking in Lawrence. I arrived at 5:15 a.m.

I had fun at Lawrence. The Phi Gams entertained me at dinner: squabs etc. then escorted me to the ball. They were cocks of the walk. The Chancellor introduced me by saying Dad was an alumnus. Many of

my family had been students and "two of my grand-
fathers had been regents." I wondered how many he
thot I had.

A

Rye, November 12, 1933

Dear Mother,

I have been getting many reactions from my appearance in Kansas. I did not know we had so many relatives and connections. I may send you another batch
of letters later.

I am going down to Philadelphia on Wednesday and
plan to see Mark Balis. He wants to know what I discovered, if anything, in Atchison.

Hastily yours,
A

Amarillo, Texas
[December 8, 1933]

Dear Mother,

Here am I, out where the west begins. I drove over
from Dallas in a borrowed car and am pushing on in
a few minutes to Lubbock — 125 miles south. I do love
the space of this country.

I sent you a package from Dallas. Also a book from
Wichita Falls. It is one I finished and thot you might
be amused to read it. It is the history of women's
underwear and is "rough" and amusing and withal his-
torically interesting. I find one omission and that is
no reference to envelope chemises. Did we not progress from panties to those circular ones with "cami-
sole" and then through teddy bears to bloomers? Send
it to the Seymour [Hotel] when you finish it . . .

I have some swell ideas which I will tell you when
next I see you. In the meantime I want you to go . . .
for a complete checkup. It may do you good to get out
of the house — even to go to a dentist . . .

Speaking of the Seymour, G.P. and I decided since
I was to be away so much and so busy in town when

at home that we could just have Allen to stay in the house and live quietly at the hotel. . .

LOL

A

Among other reasons for moving into New York was Amelia's restlessness. She was nearly thirty-seven, still slim and boyish, still the most admired woman pilot in the world, and still convinced she must go on proving it. When not lecturing, she rose early, often playing a round of golf before going to her office. Later she might fly a group of friends somewhere for lunch, and show up as the main speaker at a banquet in the evening. Otherwise she had the lectures and the fan mail, articles to write, and all the people who crowded around her wherever she appeared. At times she enjoyed this unchallenging existence, but almost cyclically she yearned for change, for something different, something dangerous, something adventurous, and above all, something to test all her strength and courage, and engage every cell, every atom of her being.

The year 1933 ended with the United States and France sharing feminine recognition in aviation, according to the Fédération Aéronautique Internationale. Amelia Earhart held first place in the records, but on her heels was Maryse Hilz, a worthy French rival, and after her came May Haizlip and Amy Mollison, Jacqueline Cochran and Ruth Nichols.

On January 11, 1934, six United States Navy planes reached Hawaii from California, after 24 hours and 45 minutes in the air. Another ocean, another first in aviation. The feat impressed Amelia. The Pacific had been first conquered by air in 1928 when Sir Charles Kingsford-Smith and his crew flew from Oakland, California, to Brisbane, Australia, and in 1931 Hugh Herndon, Jr., and Clyde Pangborn made the first nonstop transpacific flight from Samushiro Beach, near Tokyo, to Wenatchee, Washington.

So far, no one at all had successfully flown the 2400 miles between Honolulu and the mainland by himself. Or herself!

Well, why not? Why not try for another record? This time not only in competition with other women but against all comers, male and female. As soon as she could arrange it, Amelia began preparations for the first solo flight from Hawaii to California.

SIXTEEN

Pacific Solo
1934-1935

The flight was necessarily delayed a year. For one thing, the lecture schedules were already set up, and Amelia was unwilling to disappoint those who had arranged to hear her. She also needed the $250 she received for each appearance. Once when Caroline Shedd, the good family friend in Chicago, wrote asking Mrs. Earhart if Amelia would talk to her women's club, and how much she would charge, Amelia noted on the envelope: "Tell Mrs. Shedd I couldn't come for her club alone but maybe sometime when in Chicago I could come informally. Ask what they usually pay for speakers. Say I probably wouldn't charge much if it was just confined to members." Amelia was always respectful of money, and she never dealt sentimentally with it.

Then in March she had an appointment to testify before the Senate Post Office Committee, against the government's intention to deny new airmail routes to private companies and hand them over to the Army. In an interview about the same time, she suggested that government efforts should be directed toward providing "essential aids...like radio beams, night flying beacons, emergency airports, weather reporting and broadcasting...The provision of adequate flying aids should be considered no more of a subsidy than is the provision of a lighthouse thought to be a subsidy to shipping..."

Two years later, in May 1936, she would minimize the importance of aids to aviation, or appear to, when she appeared before the Senate Air Safety Committee. "I should like to have this committee make plain to the general public," she said, "that if all the aids were abandoned tomorrow, airplanes would still fly." At the time of her disappearance, little more than a year later, a good deal was made of this statement. On study, however, her contention would appear to be that nothing, not even the United States government, would or could prevent the development of aviation.

During April and the early part of May in 1934 she was lecturing in the Midwest, and then she took a swing around New England.

> Boston, [May 21, 1934]
>
> Dear Mother,
> I was so hurried here that I couldn't come out. However I am looking up plans for you on this trip to Burlington and should have something to report. I'll try to get up next week. Instead of having a couple of days in this neck of the woods, I have to fly to Albany to make a date at Pittsburgh, then drive much of the nite from there to Phila. for another engagement.
> Did you get my postcard from the Ozarks? I had a few days vacation there and had a swell time.
> A

> Hotel Seymour, New York
> May 25, 1934
>
> Dear Mother,
> I am sending you a picture of Cornelia Otis Skinner [who was a neighbor at Rye] and me in your clothes. They're not particularly good but you can get an idea of how I looked, anyway. I also am sending a copy of your marriage certificate signed by Mr. Hopkins. When I was in Burlington recently he turned up and as a surprise presented me with a duplicate. I know he would love to hear from you, if you have time to write...

I received a somewhat discouraging letter from Muriel. I hope to get up to Boston within ten days again and will definitely stop off and try to plan what should be done immediately. Please let me know when the kindergarten is out so I can concentrate on your particular affairs. I feel until school is over it is impossible to work anything out.

Sincerely yours,

A.E.

Always before, vacations had been hit or miss, a few days here or there according to the two schedules, but this year Amelia and George managed the month of August together at the dude ranch of Carl Dunrud, south of Cody, Wyoming. In 1869 this state, though still a Territory, had for the first time anywhere in the world granted women the right to vote, a circumstance which combined with the natural beauties of the Absaroka Mountains to predispose Amelia favorably toward it. For many glorious warm days on horseback and nippy nights in pitched tents resembling teepees, accompanied by guides with the gear, the Putnams packed into the heart of the mountains. When Amelia's hair grew unruly, she sat on a stump with a towel around her neck and Carl Dunrud gave her a haircut. She lounged ungracefully in the saddle sometimes, or straightened up to race her husband to the farthest pine tree. She liked Wyoming so well she made arrangements to buy property and commissioned plans for a vacation home of her own near the Dunrud ranch.

In the fall they decided to move their main base to Los Angeles. Amelia's plane needed an overhaul, and being close to the Lockheed factory would simplify preparations for the Hawaii flight. And then too, George's position with Paramount Pictures required him to spend time in California. A move seemed a sensible thing to do.

In 1934 the air was still clear over the Los Angeles basin because the highways were only two-lane cement blocks joined by tar seams, and the automobile was a luxury most families could not afford. Eucalyptus and palm trees shaded city streets and under them flamed poinsettias near oleanders, hibiscus, and Bird-of-Paradise. The Putnams usually stayed at the Ambassador Hotel, but this year they rented a bungalow at 10515 Valley Spring Lane near Toluca Lake in North Hollywood, an exclusive area where residents paid five dollars a month for the Hollywood patrol to guard their property and protect their privacy.

The location was ideal, with a golf course a mile or two away and the Lockheed factory at Burbank not far beyond. Near neighbors and friends of both Amelia and George were Paul and Myrtle Mantz. He was thirty-one, a former Army pilot who had graduated as an aviation cadet at March Field, Riverside, just at the end of World War I. When George persuaded Paramount to make *Wings* in 1928, the first big aviation movie, he hired Mantz and his fleet of planes for dogfights in the film. *Wings* won the first Academy Award for best picture of the year. In spite of a cocky swagger, Mantz's scientific approach and unquestioned skill as a stunt flyer made him exceedingly helpful to Amelia as her adviser and consultant.

California suited both Putnams. On weekends they might visit the western film star William S. Hart at his ranch, driving between orange groves past brush-covered hills studded with yucca candles, and the Sierra Madre towering in the background as they neared Newhall. Or they might attend a formal dinner at Pickfair given by Mary Pickford and Douglas Fairbanks, senior, for visiting royalty. America's Sweetheart and Lady Lindy became close friends, and at one time they considered making a film together. Will Rogers and Amelia were friends, and through him the Putnams met Will and Ariel Durant, whose monumental *The Story of Civilization* was in process; Volume 10 would win the Pulitzer Prize. An old pilot friend Wiley Post was in Hollywood, and there were others, new as well as old, plus those who were passing through or came to visit.

Sometimes they flew over sleepy little undiscovered Palm

Springs on their way to Indio for a long weekend of swimming and horseback riding with Jacqueline Cochran and her financier husband Floyd Odlum, founder of the Atlas Corporation. Jacqueline was devoted to Amelia; and Amelia was so fond of Floyd that she dedicated *Last Flight* to him.

At this point Amelia appeared to be well settled into marriage, her plans for the Hawaii flight in late December or early January were proceeding satisfactorily, and her mother was finally persuaded temporarily to leave the Morrissey family in Medford and come to North Hollywood for a long visit.

Amy Earhart blossomed in the excitement around Amelia. Her daughter's friends became her friends, and for the rest of her life, she heard from them at intervals: Paul Mantz, the Odlums, Louise Thaden, Blanche Noyes, and members of the Ninety-Nines, among those who loved Amelia. Despite her poor hearing she managed to keep a conversation going with nods and smiles, and whatever lipreading she had been able to teach herself. Then at times she withdrew to keep up her correspondence with people she had written to all her life, sometimes mailing as many as fifty letters a day and often receiving that number or more in return from Midwesterners who at one time or another had met the Otises or the Earharts, or who had called themselves to Amy's attention because of Amelia. Many continued to write lovingly after Amelia disappeared. Of course, she wrote often and at length to Pidge and the children.

On November 27, George telephoned Amelia from New York with bad news. An empty water boiler had overheated and exploded, causing a fire which destroyed one wing of the house at Rye. Priceless furnishings and all of the Rockwell Kent paintings were gone, although a collection of old and rare books was saved. As George said over the telephone, "Everything in the dining room was destroyed, the silver is a shapeless mass in a pile of ashes which was our rosewood buffet." Many of Amelia's papers from schooldays to Denison House, including school diplomas, letters, and verses, were in a small wooden box that burned.

Her trophies, however, all the medals and decorations, the awards and citations, were in a suitcase that her husband had placed in a New York bank vault for safekeeping during their California residence. A year later for Christmas, when the Rye house had been repaired, he gave her an exquisitely carved teakwood trophy chest commissioned from master craftsmen.

Just before Christmas of 1934, Amelia and George with Paul and Myrtle Mantz sailed from Los Angeles for Honolulu aboard the *Lurline,* leaving Amy at the house in North Hollywood. Amelia's bright red Lockheed Vega was covered and tied down on the aft deck, to the intense interest of the other passengers.

> At sea, December 25, 1934
>
> AT THIS FESTIVE SEASON WE WOULD EXPRESS APPRECIATION OF THE CORDIAL RELATIONS BETWEEN US AND EXTEND TO YOU BEST WISHES FOR CHRISTMAS AND THE NEW YEAR - AMELIA GEORGE.

> On board, December 26, 1934

Dear Mother,

How did you like our cablegram on Christmas? It was number 17 on the prepared list and we couldn't resist sending it. Who do you suppose composes those terrible ready made messages for the cable and wire companies?

The voyage is getting tropical-er and tropical-er. Today we breakfasted in pajamas on our sun porch. It seems impossible that yesterday was Christmas. I suppose when we land tomorrow we shall slip on grass skirts and never leave the island paradise (Chamber of Com merce, travel agencies, press are worse than California species). Nevertheless, I have enjoyed this trip more than any other water jaunt.

I am not fond of boats but this has not been bad. Possibly because of the locale and accommodations. Still I prefer the desert.

We have warmed the motor up twice and it has barked a cheerful "howdy" each time. The plane is perched on the aft tennis deck and excites considerable interest. A couple of elderly ladies are sure it's going to be flown off the ship and they are planning to be on hand for the event.

Judge Lindsey and family are on board. I was glad to meet him personally after knowing him through debates and books so long. He is very nice. [Judge Benjamin Barr Lindsey advocated trial marriage.] Ex-Ambassador Houghton [?] is also on board and a few well known Island people. Of course there are comparatively few passengers because of the holiday season.

Speaking of Christmas. Did you find your gifties O.K.? I meant to tell you I was making you a member of the Book of the Month Club. My indisposition of the night before leaving wrecked everything the last hours.

The radio on the plane has been working wonderfully. At midnight I could pick up and talk to regular airway stations. Kingman Arizona heard perfectly. Such reception is unusual for those Dept. of Commerce stations are low power and only supposed to carry a couple hundred miles. The operator on the ship is much interested and has been very cooperative as have the crew and officers.

If all goes well Paul and Myrtle will be back in about ten days, I think. They will just stay to help me and until the next boat sails. I'll have G.P. cable you when I start. My hope is to go on east if I can so I shall not see you until later if that plan materializes. Reporters may call on you. If so, be pleasant, admit you're my mother if you care to, and simply say you're not discussing plans. If they ask what you think of my doing such things, say what you think. It's better to do what [you?] want — etc.

I am enclosing $25 in case you run short. If anything comes up cable us collect — Royal Hawaiian Hotel Honolulu.

Please try to have a good time. You have had so
many squashed years, I know it's hard to throw them
off. But it can be done. I'd like you to take this trip
and I am going to plan to that end.

G.P. said you were an awfully good sport to stay
alone in the little house. I said I had known that a
long time.

I have taken possession of the stuff in the zipper com-
partment of my briefcase. Put it away until I turn up
and if I don't — burn it. It consists of fragments that
mean nothing to anybody but me.

I'll try to drop a line from the Islands but can't
promise. Anyway this will go back on the *Mariposa*
tomorrow so you ought to get it within a few days.

Cheerio in case you don't get another letter before
I hop off. I shan't go unless I am as satisfied as I can
be with all details.
                                          A.

Amelia's flight was adversely regarded, both in the Islands and
on the mainland. As recently as the past November, Captain
Charles T. P. Ulm with two Australian companions had flown
out of Oakland bound for Honolulu and disappeared somewhere
off Oahu after one feeble SOS. For twenty-seven days Navy and
Army planes, Navy surface ships, Coast Guard vessels, and scores
of fishing boats plowed crisscross paths in a fruitless hunt for any
survivors. The Coast Guard cutter *Itasca*, which would later be
prominent in the futile search for Amelia, was the last to give
up on Captain Ulm and his crew.

On December 29, with Paul Mantz already testing the plane
at Wheeler Field, Army airmen, according to the Honolulu *Star-
Bulletin*, were uneasy. "... There is nothing intelligent about flying
solo from Hawaii to the mainland," the newspaper reported. "Even
if she is successful, nothing beyond what is known would be
proved. If she fails, the ghastly Ulm search would be repeated."

In response, George Putnam said, "Go ahead and say what

you like. We will go ahead in our quiet way." Amelia said nothing. She was busy conferring with Paul, checking out the plane herself, swapping chat and "ground flying" with friendly Army pilots, and sunning and swimming whenever she could manage a free moment for the beach at Waikiki. She made only one public appearance, speaking at Farrington Hall at the University of Hawaii on the subject of "Flying for Fun."

When the Navy refused clearance for the flight on the grounds that the plane's radio lacked sufficient range for safety, Amelia protested that she had contacted Kingman, Arizona, while aboard the ship. The Navy was adamant until Paul took the plane up to 12,000 feet and spoke with Kingman himself. Then the Navy was forced to clear the flight.

The worst criticism erupted over Amelia's competition for the $10,000 prize offered by a group of businessmen, including sugar cane and pineapple growers. Since legislation was under consideration in Congress to reduce the sugar tariff, it was clear to some people that Amelia had "sold her soul" to the sugar interests. Contemptuously, she informed the sponsors at an emergency meeting that she intended "to make the flight with or without" their support. There was, she said, "an aroma of cowardice" in the room. The sponsors promptly renewed their offer of the prize money.

Everything finally came together except the weather, which was too spotty to trust but did not prevent a day's excursion to the Big Island of Hawaii, where as other visiting dignitaries always do, Amelia planted a banyan tree in Hilo.

Honolulu, January 6, 1935

Dear Mother,

I have meant to write before but days have gone and I couldn't. We have been unbelievably busy — ducking many more entertainments than accepting. The work on the plane has gone along well so far and it looks as if a weather break will occur in a few days. We have spent much time at the fields as you can imagine.

Yesterday we took our only sight seeing tour over the islands. Inter Island Airways president was our host and we visited the volcano on Hawaii. It was exceedingly interesting, tho not in eruption. One could see the different lava flows in many places and we were taken through a lava "tube" overgrown on the outside by moss and huge ferns. It was a cave built by the cooling lava and hidden until discovered years later. There are many about, some known and some unknown. Sometimes they run uphill like great organ pipes. They are as different from limestone caves as can be.

This trip and riding in an outrigger canoe with Duke Kahanamoku (the once great Hawaiian swimmer) are about the extent of our adventures except work and basking in the sun. The climate is much less tropical than I imagined. We sleep under a blanket at night and the day has no oppressive humidity. Of course everything grows luxuriantly but not jungle-y.

We have been very fortunate in being guests of Chris Holmes a wealthy cultivated "playboy" friend of Paul's. He is not here but insisted we stay at *one* of his homes. It is much better than any hotel with a staff of beautifully trained Japanese servants and everything perfectly appointed. We have lived like kings...with no bother about anything. Mr. Holmes has homes over the world ready at any time to receive any number of his friends. He is a perfect host!

The house is right on famous Waikiki beach — a really beautiful spot. In fact I believe the C of C in Honolulu is the only one to tell of the beauties of a certain spot and be right.

I hope you have been getting on alright. It seems as if we left long ago — so much has happened.

G.P. and I wonder whether we'll ever be satisfied with only one or two servants again after so many here.

Arrival after solo transatlantic flight. Culmore Ireland. 1932.

Special medal presented by Herbert Hoover. June. 1932.

Zonta Club members at a coffee shop after a formal banquet.
Springfield, Massachusetts. 1934.

(The New York News)

Ticker tape parade down Broadway to City Hall. New York. 1932.

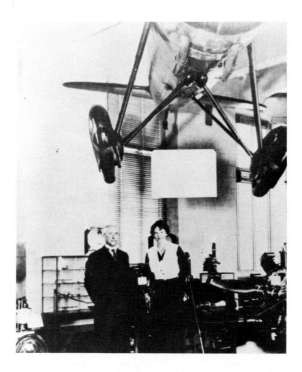

Orville Wright and Amelia Earhart at Franklin
Institute. Philadelphia. 1936.

Amelia Earhart and Paul Mantz plotting round-the-
world flight. Hollywood. 1937.

George Palmer and Amelia Earhart Putnam. Rye, New York. 1935.

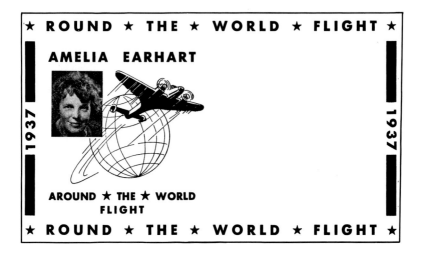

Round-the-World Flight stamped envelopes. First and second take-offs.

(Courtesy of Jean L. Backus)

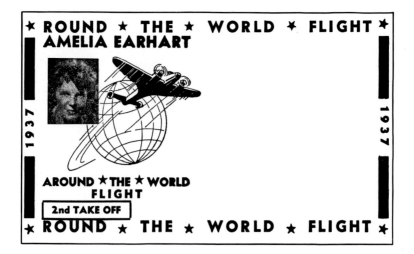

Curtis Bliss, Amelia Earhart, Fred Noonan and Gerald Bliss at Miami
Airport. May 31, 1937.

Memorial marker on Howland Island. 1937.

Amy Otis Earhart.

We think Talio will not be sufficient for our needs now.

Cheerio

A.

Five days later, few people were on hand to see the start of Amelia's "great hop" on January 11. Because of strong winds and torrential rain on Friday morning and in the early afternoon, only a small crowd of Army people living at the post gathered to watch what had been announced as another test flight.

Earlier Amelia and George with Lieutenant E. W. Stephens, the meteorology officer, several Army officials, and the Mantzes had lunched at the home of Lieutenant and Mrs. George H. Sparhawk at Wheeler Field. Then Amelia had taken a nap and Paul had gone to check out the plane and make ready for a test hop. Or so George said when asked.

About four o'clock, when Amelia and George arrived at the field, Paul had the plane out and the motor warmed up and idling. With 500 extra gallons of gas, plus additional radio and navigational aids, the Lockheed weighed over three tons. This time also, Amelia carried a bright red inflatable vest and an inflatable raft, just in case. At the field she donned a warm flying suit, and climbed a ladder to clamber into the crowded cockpit. A number of officers watched as enlisted men held the wheel chocks. "There was an obvious effort on the part of Amelia and her husband to avoid looking at each other on the field," the Associated Press Chief W. M. Ewing wrote in the *Star-Bulletin*. "They had quite evidently said their farewells before leaving Lt. George H. Sparhawk's home."

As a matter of fact, there had been more than "Aloha" to Amelia's goodbyes. On January 8 she had written a letter to George, saying in part that she was "familiar with the hazards," and believed her equipment was in the best condition. "If I do not do a good job it will not be because the plane and motor are not excellent nor because women cannot fly..."

At 4:30 P.M., Amelia settled into the cockpit, listened to the motor, gunned it, then let it idle while she watched her instruments, and finally gunned it again. The ground crew holding the blocks in front of the wheels "watched her expectantly while the big red ship thundered and trembled." Finally she waved her hand, the crew jerked the blocks, and the plane began to roll, followed by two automobiles. George was in one and Army officers in the other. They tracked Amelia as she lined up the field, gunned the motor, and at 4:44 P.M. opened the throttle.

Slowly the ship started toward the end of the runway 6000 feet ahead, where an ambulance and fire truck waited. The wheels sank inches deep into mud, Ewing wrote, which was "flung by the propeller in a stream behind, and the plane lumbered from side to side as it gathered speed." No more than 3000 feet from the start, Amelia hauled back on the stick and the Lockheed abruptly left the ground. It appeared about to sink again, and then slowly began to rise. Finally she was airborne, in a major effort to be not only the first woman but the first person ever to fly solo across any part of the Pacific Ocean and, in addition, the first solo flyer over both Atlantic *and* Pacific.

When word flashed from Honolulu to the world that Amelia Earhart had taken off for California, sky watchers began to count the hours and minutes. Navy and commercial radio stations monitored her radiophone messages, which came at frequent but irregular intervals. To everyone's dismay, she declined to give her position. She reported her altitude and speed, the two ships — Matson's *Maliko* and Dollar's *President Pierce* — that she saw, commented on the moon and stars, and invariably added that everything was okay. Once she said she could see Catalina Island clearly, which seemed to put her too far south, and someone thought it was Santa Cruz Island off Santa Barbara which she saw. Whatever the island, she saw it while she was enjoying a Metropolitan Opera broadcast from New York.

In Burbank, Lieutenant Commander Clarence S. Williams, who had plotted her course and the alternatives, fretted to know which of several landing spots she would choose. She could fly nonstop to Washington, D.C., which she secretly hoped to do, or she could land at Salt Lake City. But he thought Burbank or Oakland was more likely. To George Putnam and Paul Mantz in Honolulu and to Amy Earhart in North Hollywood, it didn't matter where she landed, just so she did.

To the thousands around the San Francisco Bay Area who were alerted by radio bulletins, it was important to learn that Amelia's signal was getting weaker according to KFI in Los Angeles, even as KPO San Francisco said it was getting stronger. The Coast Guard, on hearing this, sent four cutters to fan out beyond the Golden Gate in case she needed any assistance.

On January 12 at the Oakland Airport on Bay Farm Island, 10,000 people waited for Amelia, but when a red high-winged monoplane came in low and fast, without circling the field, and landed far down the runway nobody at first realized she was there. Then the field siren went off, and Amelia gunned the ship and turned it around toward the hangar. Now the shouting, surging mob broke police lines and rushed the plane. Catastrophe seemed certain. But Amelia maneuvered the Lockheed safely up to the hangar doors and stopped.

The cockpit popped open and, smiling, she stood up and looked out. "I'm tired," she said, and reached for a comb in her pocket though her short light hair was unruffled. The people screamed and shouted and crowded around the plane, laughing and crying and thrusting bouquets of American Beauty roses at her, trying to shake hands, jumping up to touch the sleeve of her flying suit, picking at the skin of the plane for a souvenir. Later Amelia would say, "That landing is something I shall never forget. It is in the diary of my heart. It has made Oakland my favorite airport and one of my favorite cities."

At the moment she said nothing more, or if she did it was lost in the general noise and confusion surging all around as far as she could see. Then the hangar doors opened and mechanics grabbed the wings of her plane and tugged it inside. They locked the doors quickly to prevent souvenir hunters from destroying the ship. Amelia climbed down on shaky legs, and a police escort took her off to a hotel in Oakland. At 9:15 that night, she filed a telegram to her mother: SEE YOU SOMETIME GP ARRIVES THURSDAY CHEERIO - A. Then she went to bed. She was tired, yes, but the records she had reached for were well and truly hers now.

SEVENTEEN

Records Upon Records 1935

Amelia's departure from Oakland on Sunday was an anticlimax. When she tried to take off, the weight of gas remaining in her tanks caused the Lockheed to bog down in a soggy spot at the end of the runway. When two airfield trucks failed to budge the plane, a tractor was brought in to drag it from the mud. Delayed an hour or more, and with hardly anybody watching, Amelia finally took off for Los Angeles.

Radio spread the word, however, and 2000 people greeted her at the Burbank Airport when she landed. Mrs. Earhart was not present, and Amelia said she didn't expect her mother. In fact, she added, "I didn't expect anyone to be here to meet me." To a Los Angeles *Times* reporter, she appeared genuinely surprised and pleased at the welcome. For an hour she posed for photographers, spoke into a microphone for the newsreels, and consulted with the weather observers. There was speculation that she might take off for Washington without a longer stop, but finally she consigned her plane to the field attendants and drove home with friends.

Later Amy would relate how Amelia, when she was dead tired, would say, "No talkee, Mother, my cocoa, goodnight." And doubtless she said much the same thing that night as she took her cup of chocolate to her room and went to bed. There was little time for relaxing in the days that followed, however, for

169

her renown again burgeoned overnight. From all over the world congratulations came in by telephone and telegraph while letter mail arrived in sacks. The demand for lecture dates was staggering.

Probably the Honolulu flight marked a reversal in the marital relation. Previously Amelia's fame was equally due to her own unquestioned achievements and the promotional stunts and decisions of her husband, to whom she occasionally referred as "the management." Now that changed. From the moment she arrived in Oakland the Amelia Earhart legend generated its own momentum, nourished by the courageous spirit and genuine heroism of the woman herself. There would be few if any more commercial stunts — only true accomplishments.

On Thursday George arrived from Honolulu and Amelia went out with the quarantine boat to the *Lurline* when it anchored in Los Angeles Harbor. She did not protest when a reporter called her Mrs. Putnam, since meeting her husband had nothing to do with her career. On Saturday the couple flew to Oakland for a civic dinner in her honor with state and military officials among those present, and the next day, the couple continued on to New York.

In early 1935, having completed the strenuous flight from Honolulu to Oakland, Amelia was already planning the two Mexican flights, and setting out on a strenuous lecture tour without a chance to rest. In June the combined stresses of all three flights would generate so much discomfort that she would enter Cedars of Lebanon Hospital in Los Angeles for another session with her sinuses. She was "tired of being beaten up with washings out," she would write Amy; and even after she left the hospital, her convalescence was complicated by a backache that turned into pleurisy. While it would be unwise positively to diagnose this and previous illness as the result of psychic and emotional pressures in Amelia Earhart, it is impossible to dismiss them as unconnected to the extraordinary demands she made on herself, to lack of sleep, a slim diet — only a can of tomato juice in one twenty-four-hour period during a flight — and to the mental and emotional fluctuations of those crucial hours alone in the atmosphere when she was totally responsible for her body and her machine. If nothing else, those hours were the super-human measure of her achievements.

In March the lecture tour hadn't yet begun, and she was in Washington, D.C.:

> The White House, March 4, 1935
>
> Dear Mother,
>
> I am so sorry I haven't had any time to write you before. I returned to N.Y. and found myself signed for the most strenuous lecture engagement ever under-taken. A few days out and I came here to speak at National Geographic.
>
> Mrs. Roosevelt asked me to stay at the White House overnight — then to make it headquarters until Tues-day when I leave for New England. It has been quieter here than some other places tho my schedule doesn't give one much chance to rest anywhere...
>
> I hope to start west the middle of this month. I speak in L.A. on the 30th. GP has left Paramount and is in a state trying to decide what alley he will run down. There are so many things to do.
>
> Here is a small check for your birthday. I'll do it properly later. Keep your ties and clothes cleaned. Mr. Keely will charge and if you're short send me the bill. Paul Mantz will stand by in an emergency. I hope you had him check the car. I am so sorry it broke down just when it was needed.
>
> Pidge and Albert have had to give up their house. I'll tell you about that later too.
>
> A

Between her own preoccupations and Mrs. Earhart's prolonged stay in California, Amelia's concern with the Morrissey family had subsided. Because the Putnams intended to give up their rented Hollywood house after the next adventure, however, she agreed that Amy should go back to Medford and give the unhappy Muriel a hand with the grandchildren. En route she would visit friends and relatives in the Midwest.

The President of Mexico had invited Amelia to visit his country, and she was enthusiastically absorbed in plotting a course and making her usual careful preparations for the flight. Lindbergh had flown from Washington, D.C., to Mexico City in 1927, and now Amelia could set two records at once: from Los Angeles to the Mexican capital and from there to Newark.

When the Mexican government proposed a special postage stamp, George peddled 780 autographed covers to help finance the flight. Some stamp dealers in the United States and abroad questioned the integrity of the project, however. Already in Mexico to wait for Amelia, he had to make a public statement personally guaranteeing their exclusive authenticity.

The covers were aboard the Vega when, just before midnight on April 19, Amelia took off from Burbank. She later wrote of moonlight over Baja California and the Gulf as far as Mazatlán, where she turned east over the high central mountains and plateaus of the interior. Fifty miles short of Mexico City she landed in an arid pasture near a village named Nopala, uncertain of where she was and why she hadn't reached her destination. After the astonished peons directed her in sign language, she dodged the cactus and prickly pear dotted all around what was actually a dry lake bed, and flew on to the capital, where President Lázaro Cárdenas waited with George at Valbuena Airport to welcome her.

Officially Amelia was the guest of the government, but it was the hospitable upper-class social element who vied to give more and bigger fiestas in her honor, at the same time that the American colony attempted to outdo the Mexicans. Amelia tried but failed to arrange a meeting with working women in order to investigate for herself conditions of independence and opportunities for self-support under the new Cárdenas regime.

George went back to New York and Amelia was anxious to follow, but for eighteen days Doc Kimball continued to send reports of unfavorable weather over the Gulf of Mexico. Once she went out to the Lake Texcoco mudflats to look on as soldiers contrived three miles of runway to accommodate her heavily loaded plane on a takeoff which would be doubly difficult because of the thin air at nearly 8000-foot altitude.

On May 7 from the Hotel Ritz she wrote to Amy, now with the Morrisseys in Medford, but all she said was: "I know you must be broke. Here's $20. I hope it reaches you all right. LOL. A."

Just after midnight on Wednesday, May 8, Amelia received good weather news from Dr. Kimball, and went at once to see her plane gassed up, and to watch as a Pan American Airways mechanic checked out the engine. At 6:00 A.M. Mexican time, she sent the Vega down the new runway at 100 miles per hour, and after a long and slow start was finally airborne and headed across the Gulf of Mexico. Fourteen hours and 19 minutes later, she landed at Newark Airport, 2185 miles to the north. "Everything," she later wrote, "worked as it should."

As her plane stopped rolling a frenzied crowd mobbed it, and friendly police officers nearly tore her limb from limb trying to save her. Once Amelia had defended Colonel Lindbergh when he was criticized for rudeness to a mob. Now she understood better than ever how it was to have things literally stolen off her back. The success of the two flights overwhelmingly emphasized female capability in the field of aviation, a proposition more compelling even than Amelia's personal need to compete with men, and being mobbed by one's fans was the price one paid.

New York, [May 19, 1935]
Dear Mother,
I am glad you wrote as I was getting a little worried. Isn't it horrid you were sick? I am sure with you it wasn't due to "the long air ride" [from Kansas City to Boston].

I *have* been pretty busy since the trip. My schedule as far as I can see it now is as follows:

May 23   Chicago
           Washington
May 26   Atlanta (degree at Oglethorpe)
May 28   Mexican Dinner NY
May 29–30 Indianapolis (Honorary Referee)
May 31   Muncie (Speech)

Back home until I have to start flying west to be in Atchison for June 7 Kansas editors' convention. Tulsa on the tenth and then points west. Paul Mantz and I have a lot to do together. When GP can get west I do not know. He is in the midst of a book, and picture negotiations which will keep him east indefinitely. We are still hoping to get to Wyoming July and August. If so I want you to come. If we can't make this, what would you like to do? I don't want you to get all run down at the Morrissey mansion.

We have rented our house for a year and so are shed of that responsibility while we are in our present state. A doctor, specialist in the chest cavity. They have much of their own furniture so we didn't have to replenish the whole.

Please send me Rats Lice etc. GP's mother wants to read it.

I am glad you had a nice time at Cains [in Kansas City]. I'll probably see the gang when I go to Atchison.

I slipped up on Mammytide, but expect a package later. By the way I paid Dr. Severy. That's all, ain't?

My plane is in Beantown but I don't know whether I'll get up to fetch it myself or not. I'll let you know anyway.

                    Cheerio
                       A

                              Los Angeles, [June 25, 1935]
Dear Mrs Eho,
    Yes, here I am again [Cedars of Lebanon Hospital].

The sinus is kicking up and I am tired of being beaten up with washings out so Dr. Goldstein is going to work on me tomorrer.

By the way, my name should be Engelheim or Earhartbaum. Of course the institution is Jewish but has the highest standing around here as so often everywhere.

I spoke last night in Pasadena. Enclosed is the check. I am terribly sorry I have been unable to arrange a summer for you but — plans have been so unsettled I couldn't. Use the $250 for 3 weeks near at hand for Pidge and the children and you. If you or they have to have a few little clothings get 'em at Filene's and send me the bill. That's all I can do. You need some white shoes and a simple white dress, I know. Get some low heeled shoes for beach wear. If you can't get ones like your brownies send me the size and I'll get 'em here. Also for Pidge.

GP is coming here some time. We may get to Wyoming but it's so uncertain with my trouble here I can't tell.

I'll write you later.

Cheerio,

A

Sorry you ain't here.

Los Angeles, [July 5, 1935]

Dear Mother,

I got your wire all right and the letter came this morning.

I left the hospital as soon as I could as usual, and went to Mrs. Lighton's. There a backache I had which I thot was a strained muscle turned into pleurisy. I am still in bed with my side strapped. GP arrived yesterday, which helps. I am getting on now and can get up as soon as 3 days pass in which I run no temperature. The nose is healing O.K. though I am warned I'll have a headache for another week!

You can always reach me thru Paul Mantz. I'll probably be here for a month or more now. Whether G.P. and I get to Wyoming is a problem still.

About your vacation. I strongly advise your getting as near Boston as possible to save car fare. Also for any trips to town necessary.

I should rather you take a place for a shorter time and have a real rest, not a cheap hole where there are things to put up with. *For instance, I do not want you and Pidge to do house work. In fact I forbid that.* Find some place where meals are served nearby.

About clothes. Please remember you and Pidge attract attention as my relatives so spare me blowsies. I'd prefer you to get a few simple decent clothes, both of you. Not awful cheepies, so people who don't look below the surface won't have anything to converse about. Things you get now are cheaper and can be used next year.

I hope you get near the sea but a good country place would be O.K. Get listings of good places. Women's Exhange carries them I am sure. *Don't let Pidge just bungle around...* Put an ad in the paper and be sure you have a desirable dugout, even if it takes a week longer to discover. Can't you go Marblehead? I am sorry I couldn't help this year with details.

I had quite a doings at Atchison. I suppose Mary has written you...

L.O.L.

A

What do you mean your throat swollen? What sense is there in neglecting health? You know I want you to be treated whenever necessary. *See a doctor and write me.* You may be a menace to the children besides yourself. I never heard of such stuff. ! ! ! ! ! ! !

X ? X — — —

Los Angeles, [July 28, 1935]

Dear Mother,

This is the handbill which advertised my Pasadena

lecture [June 23, 1935].

Today we bought a small house here! GP has been letting off steam since he arrived, how he could not leave the east, etc. etc. But Paul and I have kept him so busy with the funny businesses we have stirred up that his bleat has grown less and less. Imagine my surprise when day before yesterday he asked me to drive him around the Toluca Lake district — where he had been busy pointing out the impossibilities of even renting even for a short time.

Well, at the very end of Valley Spring Lane (I don't know whether you ever walked there or not) was a little house with a "For Sale" sign on it. It was a square lot with two sides on the golf course and a hundred foot lot on the other, now vacant. We got home and he said, "I think I'll just call up that real estate man and see what he has to say." The result was in four minutes we were seeing the place and next day made an offer for it. GP left at one today via United and actually two minutes before the plane took off the real estate man rushed up and reported our offer accepted. Whew!

A good many changes will have to be made in the house, for it is ill-arranged, but cute on the outside. I'll send you some pix soon.

I am going into business with Paul Mantz in United Air Services. My ship is still undergoing repairs, that is repainting and re-upholstering and when it is finished I shall put it in with his fleet for charter. We are going to have a school and plan all kinds of things. GP is as excited as we are.

I am coming east to speak at Chatauqua on the ninth. Then I shall be around NY until the fifteenth. I speak at Lakeside, Ohio, just outside Cleveland on the seventeenth. Then home here until I hev to start my heavy schedule in October. I will give you the dope on that after it is thoroughly jelled. It is a Tartar.

Maybe we shall try an air circus in September. It

looks pretty much as if we would at Grand Central Airport. A new kind, with no races but just unusual stunts. GP will come back and handle the publicity and supply the drive and some ideas. He is all hep about this too.

I enclose a paper he had printed as a joke on the Lightons. Their ranch is near Oceanside and as I told you GP and I went there for several days before they came down for the week end. We were both so tired that we could not keep awake and in town they had teased us about sleeping sickness. So we drove into Oceanside before they came in order to have some terrible yellow quarantine signs printed. We tacked them up all over the ranch.

SLEEPING SICKNESS BY ORDER

OF THE BOARD OF HEALTH.

When GP got into the little newspaper office where the job was done he could not resist fixing up the local blatter. Dorothy Parker and her husband Allan [sic] Campbell and the Mantzes were to be guests so he wrote what he could in the short time we had and asked the editor to insert it in the regular edition after his quantity had gone out. The cuts were dug out of old files that no one had opened in years. It was a great success.

You speak of leaving Rockport July fifteenth. Is that decision due to money or lease? If money, how much more until August first? Let me know immediately.

I'll try to write more adventures soon. I want this to make the four o'clock TWA plane this afternoon.

Yr. doter

A

Neither the charter service nor the aviation school with Paul Mantz came to anything, and in the end, even the air circus planned for September was abandoned. There simply wasn't any time for them, not when the demand for lecture dates never let up. The spring schedule had been heavy, in the fall it was doubled.

Furthermore, in June Amelia had accepted an appointment as counselor and adviser in aeronautics at Purdue University, Lafayette, Indiana. She was expected to spend a month in residence each year, and this year would go in November to confer with women students on their careers.

During August, Amelia was mostly at the Burbank Airport with Paul Mantz, either flying or discussing at length the around-the-world flights of her good friend Wiley Post. He had followed the Arctic Circle nonstop with Harold Gatty in 1931, and the same course alone in 1933. Now he and Will Rogers were about to take off on another Arctic Circle flight.

Probably Amelia told Paul Mantz, if no one else, the dream of her own world flight at the Equator, a distance of 25,000 miles or more. Her route would be longer than Post's and more hazardous; it would require more preparation and planning than any flight she or anyone else had ever undertaken. It would be the most ambitious aviation attempt in history. And the most costly. But she was determined to make it — if and when she could get the money, forty or fifty thousand probably, to start.

On Sunday, August 11, Amelia and George were guests at the Will Rogers ranch in Santa Monica, along with Wiley Post, the Fred Stones, and the Will Durants. On Thursday, August 15, Wiley Post and Will Rogers died when the *Winnie Mae* crashed in dense fog near Point Barrow, Alaska.

Amelia grieved deeply for the cowboy humorist and the noted aviator, and mixed with her sorrow was the guilt common to survivors when those emotionally close to them perish. Among the symptoms are nightmare, insomnia, anxiety and depression states, and other mental-emotional imbalances, while physically the survivor may have nonspecific complaints of gastrointestinal dysfunction, rheumatism, or neuralgia. Although Amelia had not survived a disaster of mortal potential, she and other flyers risked their lives every time they left the ground, and the trauma was consistent with the special camaraderie of all airmen and women. Amelia hid her grief as she always hid powerful emotions, and filled her lecture date at Lakeside, Ohio, on August 17. She then returned to California and the new house on Valley Spring Lane until time for the National Air Races to Cleveland over Labor Day.

EIGHTEEN

Sisters
1935-1936

[In flight, September 4, 1935]

Dear Mother,

Paul G.P. Al Menasco and I have just left Denver and are now flying by Pike's Peak. You should see it from the air onct. I remember your stories of riding up it. Now you can see a couple of motor roads and some little buildings on top. I have never been so near in the daytime. It is pretty bald, kind of pinkish above timber line. The valleys to the left are filled with fog very white in that bright sun. Paul is flying as he knows the country here better than I do.

We are returning from Cleveland whence we went in the Bendix [air races]. We had no more intention of going than you, but we got to figuring pilots' chances and decided we would win fifth place against ships 50–90 miles faster than Lockheed. So we cranked up and cruised along and won $500. Enough to pay our expenses. We had fun. Old Bessie the fire horse came through.

Change of subject

I wish you would send me for the vegetable concentrate man samples for urine analysis of both children Pidge and you. Get 4 small bottles at drug store ready for mailing, label each and send to me. Put age of each person and medical history diseases, operations,

181

symptoms if any. [The doctor] will make up a concentrate suitable for individual needs. I think it will be
good for all of you especially if food is likely to be poor.
By the way GP is an addict now. The concentrate is
doing him lots of good.

GP expects to go back to N.Y. soon after he helps
Paul and me announce our set up. I shall stay in LA
till my lecture dates.

I am not sure how much we'll do on the house right
now. If it was left as is would you like to stay in it for
Nov & December? I'll have more dope on this later.

We hope to stop at Grand Canyon Airport for lunch.
Then on to Burbank in the afternoon.

I'll mail this there.

> Love,
> A

On September 30, Amelia began her lecture tour in Ohio at
Youngstown, and throughout October she was on one-night
stands.

> Duluth, Minnesota, [October 3, 1935]

Dear Mother,

Here's a doll which was given me. I think it's kinda
cute but I don't need it on this strenuous schedule.
This is swell country but quite diff from Cal.

> LoL
> A.E.

> Chicago, [October 12, 1935]

Dear Maw,

I spoke tother day in Lincoln Nebraska and a
Challiss came up to greet me. Mary, I think she said.
She asked about Aunt Milly and said I looked so like
her sitting on the platform. I thot she meant Grandma
but then she said she's in Calif. now. Does she mean

Cousin Amelia? and if so who is she? About 35 or less with a child of 15 or so I think...

Here's a letter I got last night. I didn't see her.

G.P. is here on his way west. We are having a day or two together. Will meet again in December.

Goo bye

A

Later when asked if people she had lost track of suddenly "popped up" because of Amelia's fame, Mrs. Earhart said they did, because as a "railroad family every promotion meant a change to another place." Distant relatives or people who claimed relationship, or old friends, as in the letter Amelia forwarded to her mother from a lady who knew Mrs. Earhart in Des Moines and "loved her dearly."

Chicago, [November 3, 1935]

Dear Maw,

Here's fifty bucks. I have been so busy I haven't had time to do anything but the treadmill.

I left my car at St. Louis, hopped an airline to K.C., picked up Cousin Rilla and her Ford and drove to Pittsburg, Kan.

Toot is on her way to the west coast and I saw her for ten mins. this A.M.

Did I tell you I stayed with Ann Park in Elkhart and drove over with Virginia [high school friend]?

Will try to write from Purdue.

A

Purdue University
[November 23, 1935]

Dear Mrs. Eho,

Enclosed is a Thanksgiving turkey of a sort. Also a copy of a questionaire [sic] I circulated here among the women students. I am just getting results today.

The work has been very interesting and has served to crystallize some of my ideas which were rather form-less before.

Please tell Pidge when I wrote her about cancelling a dinner she was planning in Cambridge, I did not mean that GP and I would not be glad to eat at home with *just the family* if she wishes. That is, if she will have a maid come in for whom I will gladly pay.

A

When it came to modern feminine education, Amelia admitted she had something of a chip on her own shoulder. ". . . I have known girls who should be tinkering with mechanical things instead of making dresses, and boys who would do better at cooking than engineering." Purdue University, with 6000 students, 1000 of them women, was more than sympathetic to this philosophy and even offered a course in "household engineering."

Actually this was not the first time Amelia had engaged in an educational project. Once she had undertaken a study of menstruation and flying, believing it obsolete to disqualify women as pilots on the grounds that "on specific occasions their physical and nervous reactions would go to pieces." She consulted women in all kinds of strenuous professions, dancers, circus performers, athletes, and believed she had information that would impress a board of medical officers. Unfortunately, she was wrong.

Nearer her heart than research was advising young women on careers. And the women of Purdue responded to her enthusiastically. It was natural they should. Loping energetically across campus, or being available in her dormitory room for evening consultation, tall and skinny Amelia Earhart, with the infectious grin and the coolly direct blue eyes, looked more like another student than a thirty-eight-year-old legend and consultant to the faculty. The girls loved her. They respected her honest and logical realism, her strong belief that women were not only entitled but obliged to break with tradition if they wished to. They saw clearly the future she told them they could make for themselves.

The questionnaire she sent around was designed to explore what plans the women had for after college, and from the results to suggest what new courses might be added and what might be dropped from the curriculum. When 92 percent of the women said they wanted to go into gainful occupation, Amelia advised them to try a certain job, to do it, and if they found something later that looked better to make a change. "And if you should find that you are the first *woman* to feel an urge in that direction, what does it matter? Feel it and act on it just the same. It may turn out to be fun. And to me fun is the indispensable part of work."

Some people criticized this last requirement. "Amelia has fun," an unknown columnist commented in 1937. "Yes, and has it her own way. . . she has flown every place and in every way that seems feasible for her, and the concerned face of her faithful husband as he tells her goodbye time and again, suffering apparently in silence, but undoubtedly suffering, touches the public sentiment. Enough fun, Amelia, enough fun."

The time Amelia spent at Purdue was interesting and she enjoyed it, but even before the month was over she was back on the lecture circuit, appearing in Frankfurt, Indiana, on November 26, Zanesville, Ohio, on the 27th, and Buffalo, New York, on the 28th. There George met her for a day or two together. The first three weeks in December were filled with lectures, right up to the 20th, and frequently she had a morning date in one place, a second date in the same city and possibly one in the evening. Or it might be that her morning and evening lectures were in different cities, sometimes many miles apart. The itinerary that has survived is awesome.

In the middle of the month, she managed a weekend visit to see Amy and the Morrisseys. Muriel was now so tightly bound into the domesticity that Amelia deplored, it was a wonder the two could communicate on any level. They did, of course, sisterly affection lubricating any awkwardness, and Mrs. Earhart was there as catalyst. In moments of desperation, if it came to that, they talked about young Amy, now four, and David, a year older.

Amelia dealt with ideas, great concepts of freedom and recognition for women accepted equally with men in aviation, and of public adoption of the airplane as a practical means of transportation. Muriel lived for her church and her teaching, and things she felt her children were entitled to: summer camp, dancing school, music lessons, horses to ride, decent birthday celebrations, and money to buy Christmas gifts. For herself, she wanted books and concerts and England. She wanted a lily on the altar for her father's birthday, and much later a lily for Amelia. Above all, she wanted a "flivver" so they could go for an outing once in a while. Neither Albert nor Amelia, who considered cars "money eaters," could see any way for the Morrisseys to acquire a car, much less maintain it.

Occasionally Muriel considered divorcing Albert. Only he was regarded as "just wonderful" by the town, the church, and his American Legion buddies, and furthermore he gave her no legal grounds. He wasn't physically cruel to her or the children, he didn't drink, smoke, or womanize, and as far as anyone knew he supported his family and was a good husband and father. Leaving him might be regarded as desertion in the courts and deprive her of alimony and child support. Anyway her pride would be destroyed if the town knew the truth. It was bad enough for Amelia and GP to know. At least she could enjoy her children and grieve for poor Amelia who had none.

If Amelia was bored in Medford, she probably didn't show it, and if Pidge thought her sister unsympathetic, she didn't say so aloud. Mrs. Earhart undoubtedly listened and nodded and confided all Muriel's problems to Amelia, making light of her own, and emphasizing what was due the great-grandchildren of Judge Otis, never mind about the Earhart side of the family.

They loved each other, these three, and Amelia always retained the sense of responsibility which she had assumed when the family moved to California. Possibly she even felt guilty for having successfully defied convention and created exactly the kind of free existence that suited her and for which she was well fitted. She would always make sure her mother was secure, and, if it came down to it, she would take care of Muriel and the children as well.

On Monday when she drove away she was probably glad to be back on her own schedule again.

Syracuse, New York
[December 17, 1935]

Dear Mother,

What a day it turned out to be from Boston — or rather night. I ran into snow and rain and icy roads and didn't get to Bing. [Binghamton, New York] until two P.M. . . . It is still bad but colder so the snow doesn't stick on the windshield.

I am enclosing a small check for your personal gifties. I left some with Pidge for the brats, but you may have some specials you'd like to get. Please don't send it *all* to Buzz and Mary [Balis]. You know I contribute every month to their upkeep...

I forgot to tell you while in Mudford that I am in the process of paying off about $3000 on Dad's hilltop. You know he was fighting that improvement case at the end and the bonds totaled more than that. The company which held them is bankrupt now...The property is not worth any more and the street paving was just a confiscatory measure which didn't work as the depression came along. The $3000 includes the purchase of half lots from old Jen Jordan and taxes on them. Her lots were ruined and Dad owned the back half.

I'll have to be going to Watertown [New York] tomorrow. I stopped halfway tonight...

L.O.L.
A

New York, [December, 1935]

Dear Mrs Eho,

I was afraid you would catch cold scuttling around after dark the way you do, so I sent some heavies. If they are too prosaic please exchange. In any case *wear*. There is a pair of slippers to match the nightie on the way. I didn't have much time to shop and my best shopper has been ill so everything is not just as ordered.

I chucked in some hairnets by the way and some Kleenex to save towels — one for you and the other for the family.

The speeches at Cortland [New York] and thereabout went very well. Sometime you will be amused to read the clippings.

About Dad's little house. There is only one but while the land once was clear there was so much assessed against it, including taxes etc etc that it really amounted to rebuying it to get a clear title.

The Nat Geog is on the way and a nize new book GP tells me. Enclosed is a joyful for you and be sure it's joyful. Mayhap a movie there are several good ones. Mutiney [sic] on the Bounty, etc.

LOL

A

Nineteen thirty-six was busier than any previous year for Amelia Earhart; by its end she had delivered nearly 150 lectures, in addition to planning and training for the world flight. In January the flight was not all that certain, so she started out in good faith to visit nine southern cities in two weeks, only to have nine more added and a third week committed to lectures.

Knoxville, Tennessee
[January 18, 1936]

Dear Mother,

This is as smoky a city as Pittsburgh. And such a

shame too, as the mountains are lovely. Enclosed is
a check. I am sorry to be so late but I have been leading
a terrific life.

G.P. meets me in Bowling Green, Ky, on Tuesday.
I am not sure whether it will be more or less strenuous
with him.

LOL

A

After the marital interlude, Amelia hurried to Nashville to meet
Blanche Noyes, an actress with the Orpheum Players, who was
an old friend and pioneer aviatrix. In the first Women's Air Derby
of 1929, Mrs. Noyes had discovered fire in the baggage compart-
ment of her plane and landed unexpectedly in Texas to put it
out. Then she took off and rejoined the race. Recently widowed,
she was going back into flying and hoped for an opening in
California. In time she would be employed by the Bureau of Air
Commerce in Washington, D.C.

From Nashville the two crossed Texas, darted up into Oklahoma, and returned to Texas, after which Amelia kept two
appointments in Tucson, Arizona. Along the way she sent her
mother a picture postcard showing the Santa Fe Railroad chain
of hotels from Chicago to the Pacific, and postmarked from the
post office aboard Train 26.

[January 28, 1936]

Do you remember Amarillo? We are lunching at Fred
Harvey's as you and I did when taking the little
Franklin west.

Cheerio,

A.E.

The two women reached California in the first week of February, and Mrs. Noyes probably exclaimed over changes at the

Burbank Airport. Now called the Union Air Terminal, it served three scheduled transport lines, United, Western, and TWA. Beyond the terminal building great cement runways spread in five directions, and immense hangars fringed the field. One of these was leased by Paul Mantz, who housed his fleet of planes there and always had room for Amelia's Vega when she flew in. Once or twice she had stayed with him and Myrtle in their Toluca Lake house near the Putnams' on Valley Spring Lane. This time she could not because Myrtle had sued Paul for divorce and named Amelia as one of the two corespondents. As far as Amelia was concerned, however, the divorce was not worth mentioning to Amy when she next wrote to her mother.

> Fort Worth, Texas, [February 25, 1936]
> Dear Mrs. Eho,
> Here am I in Ft. Worth en route to San Antonio for a speech. Then to Birmingham, St. Petersburg and Miami. I'll be in N.Y. about the eighth.
> I came on by airline, leaving my ship and auto and husband in Los Angeles.
> I sent you a pix taken at Mission Inn at Riverside (in case you thot it Bombay or somewhere east of Suez) I also sent a box of oldies for whoever can wear.
> About the vegetable compounds — I think water or fruit juice is best. After practice the taste isn't bad at all. Can't taking it be taken for granted instead of something disguised and to be urged?
> We have the plans of the little house in N. Hollywood just about completed and hope to start altering when we return to the coast in May. In the meantime have Pidge send me the bill for glasses etc so I can keep things paid on the way. I write you again en route.
> > L.O.L.
> > A
> I hope I get word from Pidge at San Antonio about the house situation there. I told her to write N.Y. as Berger [GP's secretary] would forward it.

On March 5, George wrote to reassure Mrs. Earhart concerning the Mantz divorce "mess in Los Angeles," which he attributed to a cheap lawyer's effort to create publicity by perpetrating innuendoes against Amelia. Finally Amelia herself commented briefly on the situation she had left in California.

New York, [March 23, 1936]

Dear Mrs. Eho,

I have been so busy since I reached NY that I haven't had a minute to write you. I am sorry your birthday is delayed. Anyway a few paggages will begin to trickle in shortly. Many happies.

Poor old Myrtle Mantz had to get nasty in the trial. The only two women she had not driven away from Paul paid for their loyalty by being dragged into a divorce suit. The silly accusations fell of their own weight and I cannot but feel she will eventually do something so disgraceful that the world will know what she is. Because, of course, after her self inflicted publicity she will be watched. I really have been fortunate, for any one who has a name in the paper is a target for all sorts of things.

I spoke at the YW here last evening. Tootie went along with us. She is doing very well and looks well too. My next talk is at Darby Conn. not far from where Louise de Schweintz lives. I hope to catch a glimpse of her. It has been a good many years since I have saw. Did GP send you a schedule of talks after that? I go west through Ohio and Mich. If he didn't, let us know and I'll see you get a copy.

We drove both Franklins to Calif. and now have a swell little new Terraplane, which I plan to use on the trip. It's blue and a coupe.

GP and I are pulling a party next Sunday evening. Everyone from Fanny [sic] Hurst to Frank Owen who draws Philbert for Colliers is coming. I loathe large parties but we owe so many people we thought we had oghter do something.

When I was in San Antonio who should come up but Mrs. Kennedy. She evidently is doing very well running a flower factory. She gave me a product and sent her love to you. She showed me Dorothy's little girl and asked if I remembered D. I wonder if she still pounds down on her high heels as she descends stairs.

Does the vegetable compound go down any easier. It ought to. Be sure to order more when that is gone, as it must be used over a long period for results.

LOL

A

I also saw Eliz Shedd for a minute at Birmingham, Ala.

Far more important to Amelia than these subjects was an event that occurred on March 20 in California. An order was placed with the Lockheed factory for an Electra, an advanced nonmilitary, two-motored, dual-control monoplane, capable of 210 miles per hour and 27,000-foot altitude. The plane could seat ten passengers, but Paul Mantz intended to strip it and fill it with all the latest gadgets and auxiliary fuel tanks he knew about or heard about or thought necessary or desirable. In the end, there would be more than a hundred dials and levers on the control panel, and the plane would be capable of 4500 nonstop air miles.

The Purdue University Research Foundation had put $50,000 into an Amelia Earhart Fund to purchase a "flying laboratory" for their adviser in aeronautics. The circumstance raised some eyebrows as to just what scientific use the plane would be put in the skies over Indiana, and after her disappearance many were certain the whole thing was a plot hatched by the intelligence services with University cooperation. At the time, Amelia could hardly wait to take delivery of her new airplane and start preparations for the round-the-world flight.

NINETEEN

World Flight 1936

Amelia's preparations for the flight began on paper and by telephone. Paul Mantz would be her technical adviser, and former Naval Commander Clarence S. Williams, who had charted her flight from Hawaii, would lay out and map the world route. When her friend Captain Harry Manning of the SS *President Roosevelt* volunteered his services as navigator, Amelia accepted at once. A Medal of Honor winner after a rescue at sea, Manning had given her practical instruction in navigation in 1928 on the return voyage from her first Atlantic flight. Now he was ready to take a six-month leave of absence from his ship to make the flight, because even Amelia had to admit she could not go the distance alone. The oceans she would cross were too vast and unexplored, and navigation by the stars would literally be a matter of life and death.

The itinerary took shape in her mind, or perhaps it had been there all along. From Oakland to Honolulu, then to a pinpoint in the south-central Pacific called Howland Island, and on to Australia. From there across India to Arabia, and then across Africa and the South Atlantic to Brazil. Finally north to New York, a lap she hoped to fly solo.

Preliminary planning had to include securing the necessary passport visas to land in and take off from various countries along the route, and the legal clearances to overfly them. George took on these chores, eventually spending a whole month going in person from embassy to embassy in Washington, D.C., to secure them. He also arranged to purchase stores of gasoline from Standard Oil of New Jersey, and extra parts which might be needed from Pratt & Whitney. With the advice and aid of Jacques de Sibour, a British pilot and friend, these were shipped off to selected stations along the route. Sibour, acting as agent in the Orient, also sent men capable of handling them and making the local arrangements to be in place for Amelia's arrival.

In spite of the great number of people involved, no official word of the flight leaked out until the fall when Colonel J. J. Johnson, Assistant Secretary of Commerce, mentioned it while commenting on the questionable value of what he called "stunt flights" versus experimental transatlantic mail and passenger routes already licensed by America, England, France, and Germany. At the time, Pan American was already flying on schedule to Mexico and South America over the Caribbean, and now was establishing bases for its China Clipper service between San Francisco and Hong Kong, including stops at Midway, Wake, Guam, and the Philippine Islands, the route Fred Noonan had surveyed and advised. England had its Imperial Airway routes to Egypt, India, and the Far East, and was in competition with Air France and the Dutch KLM for Southeast Asia. Around the world at the Equator was almost the only notable flight waiting to be made. When the Electra was ordered in March and gossip said that Amelia Earhart was about to make the flight, she denied it publicly as well as when next she wrote to Amy.

De Kalb, Illinois, [April 1, 1936]
Dear Mother,
April first — and the snow getting thicker and thicker. I drove all morning on icy pavements and now these are being coated with snow. Such weather. My driving tomorrow will be a long process, I suspect.
I have a grand surprize for you. I can't tell you

now but it's a swell one. When I get back I'll pop up to Medford and spring it. By the way it's nothing I'm doing. The rumor about the world flight in June is applesauce. Confidentially I shall have a new airyplane to play with then I hope, but as I'm busy lecturing until May or thereabout, I shall not hop off in June. It would take months to prepare such a trip — maybe a year.

Your letter came yesterday. Mail chases me around but I'm always glad to get it on the circuit.

Please let me know when I sent the last check. I have no files with me so forget...

I'm off to a lecture.

Cheerio

A

New York, [May 6, 1936]

Dear Mother,

If I were to send you a W.U. mammy-tide greeting it would be #400 enclosed. Please read and consider it sent.

[I'm just a little tot, I haven't much to say;
    just want to wish my mama a Happy Mother's Day.]

I have to go to Richmond Va next Monday to speak. I'll be back in N.Y. about the 14th and will probably come north to see you and unfold the great secret. I'll let you know.

This is a hasty note. I am so rushed with things piling on me since my return. I had a cold a week ago and retired to bed. Then Sec. Roper asked me to testify before a Senate Committee so I rolled out of bed and went to Washington. All in all my schedule was much upset.

L O L

A

As in 1934, her Washington appearance was before the Senate Air Safety Committee and concerned government subsidies to provide flying aids such as radio beams, beacons, and emergency airfields. Flying is accepted so widely today one hardly recalls that fifty years ago a pilot might make a forced landing in a pasture, and might only discover his location on another occasion by flying low enough to read the name on a lonely railroad station.

On April 1, Amelia had announced a "grand surprize" for Amy, and she mentioned the matter several times again, always with the promise of coming to Medford to "unfold the great secret." When she discovered that instead of being free on May 14, as she had planned, she and George were expected as overnight guests at the White House, she could hold back no longer.

> New York, [May 9, 1936]
> I can't wait to tell you
> <u>You are going abroad this summer</u>
>
> ! ! ! ! ! ! !
> with Nancy Balis as companion and hand maiden
> <u>You sail on the Westernland on June 13</u>
> It's a one class steamer of the Red Star Line. It's not a *socially* interesting ship but will probably have teachers students et al who are more humanly interesting.
>
> ---
>
> You return Aug. 3 on same ship.
> I booked passage today.
> > More later
> > Yr. doter
> > A

> Los Angeles, [after May 22, 1936]
> Dear Mother,
> Pidge says you are beautiful with your new perm. I hope you like the clothes which have come — or should have. I am paying for a washer 'ooman for Pidge so lay off that from now on, and try to be luxurious.

When you come back I want you out here. Our house will be almost finished then I hope. You won't know the district — 40 new homes have gone up in one section since we were here. We think we are going to have a very nize lil place and it looks as if we would spend more and more time in Cal. See you later.

A

[Undated and unsigned]

Suggestions and comments

On bus trip to Scotland only one suitcase is allowed. Therefore pack extra ones to check with Raymond Whit [Whitcomb, travel agents, Boston and London] or wherever they suggest. Take either the square or big brownie. Include brown suit, tan sweater, 1 dinner dress (blue long sleeve) (new) knit suit, brown silk tunic, not to mention underwear.

I have suggested all brown to conserve on shoes hats accessories. If you wish take the best brown silk dress and coat for Sunday or dinner, do so. It's rather hard on good clothes, however, to pack and drag around.

Watch cleaning and pressing. After return from trip you will need to have suit cleaned and pressed. Blue costumes will be welcome if you have been brown for 10 days. Keep shirts laundered, ties pressed and shoes shined.

Please don't down the Roosevelt administration. It's all right to be reactionary inside but it is out of step with the times to sound off about the chosen people who have inherited or grabbed the earth. You must think of me when you converse and I believe the experiments carried on today point the way to a new social order when governments will be the voice of the proletariat far more than democracy ever can be.

In all cases be careful of reporters. They may find you out. Be *cheerful* with them and smile for photographs. The serious face in real life looks sour in print. The grinning face moderately pleasant.

Don't express international opinions. Say you're on quiet visit; hope to fly across sometime; you're going to probe around; not social visit. You approve of my flying; you don't know my plans for future; mention any special things which have impressed you. (In England talk of English things, France French, etc. Don't praise Westminster in Paris.) *Look on cheerful side* never tell of mishaps, lost baggage, cold mutton chops, runs in your hose, etc.

Suggest you wear dark blue wool for departure and landing if not too warm. It looks so swell.

Order of dressiness
Brown figured silk with coat to match
blue wool with cape
brown suit
(new) brown knit
blue silk — brown silk
On the boat, the blue silk if warm in mornings is O.K. and for luncheon. Also both knits and brown silk. Suggest old suit on boat to alternate with new which is one step dressier. Laundry can be done on boat so piqué jackets can be fresh on landing if warm.

Stay in bed first day out! In any case, you may feel squeamish but don't try to fight it. *Whether or not you do stay in bed anyway.* What are your pretty nighties for? And a stewardess?

Suggest you buy a small iron abroad if practical. Am not sure about this. Enquire.

Keep manicured and have hair done every 10 days.

Use Vince after every meal more often if not feeling well. Important.

If raining don't wear kid gloves. They'll spot and be ruined. Wear washables or fabric. (If you are not adequately supplied buy a pair in London.)

I have given you very decent stockings. Also everyday ones. Keep separate. Do not wear very shears [sic] for everyday if strenuous exercise is in order. Also if lying down with knees bent loosen garters to decrease pull over knees. Do not yank *any* hose on from *top.* The blues are pretty shear but can be worn for ordinary usage. They tend to fade with too much washie. Don't try to save by not wearing, however. Remember silk rots and to get the good you must use.

Evening dresses

Most formal gray lace with blue jacket

Next blue net with white (fur jacket)

Next transformed blue nightgown (fur jacket)

This last is just a dinner dress

Save the gray for the festive night on the boat. There always is one.

In emergency refer to Raymond Whit. If you run out of cash check with them. I'll leave instructions or cable me 2 W. 45 if they unresponsive.

Don't be reactionary with Nancy. Let her be radical. Youth which isn't is pretty poor and all her family are sticks.

Last, have a good time.

Amelia's excessive concern with detail, from not downing the Roosevelt Administration to not pulling on hose from the top, is interesting; this is the total attention she gave to preparing for a long flight. Since she intended to campaign for Roosevelt's reelection, it was perhaps as well to warn Mrs. Earhart not to voice her opposition to "that man in the White House." But did Amelia seriously think Amy indifferent to or incapable of grooming herself? One wonders. The advice seems more for one's child than one's mother.

Even more interesting is Amelia's view of future governments as "the voice of the proletariat" in a new social order resulting from "experiments carried on today." This was the year of the Olympic Games in Berlin, the Nazi German reoccupation of the Rhineland, the start of the Spanish Civil War, and the flight of the Emperor Haile Selassie as Italians conquered Ethiopia.

Although it is unthinkable that Amelia would blindly endorse either fascism or communism, some ideals of either or both were apparently acceptable to her. And she was not alone. Lindbergh became so committed to speaking against war that in 1941, after Roosevelt branded him a "defeatist and appeaser," he resigned from the United States Army Air Corps Reserve. Ironically, America's greatest male flyer could only serve the United States during World War II as a civilian consultant.

Amy Earhart was no more a profound or well-informed intellectual than Amelia, but the warning was unnecessary. Traveling as "Miss Balis and her aunt," Amy and Nancy escaped publicity altogether. They were at the Park Lane Hotel in London when Amelia found time to write her mother.

Los Angeles, [July 1, 1936]

Dear Mother,

I must get this letter off or you'll be home before it reaches you. I have been so busy with the ship, with the house, with lecturing, and, alas, the last few days with GP's mother's serious illness and death, that I haven't had time to eat.

As you know I spoke before the WCTU at Tulsa. Paul flew my ship to meet me and pick up another plane at Houston. Then I persuaded a pilot friend of mine in Tulsa to come west with me for a visit knowing GP had to stay in the east a while. So — we, a party of five, went to the Dallas Centennial for a day. Then to California. The weather has been lovely so we have ridden horses and flown airplanes and I don't know where 2 weeks has gone. All the while poor Fannie has been getting weaker but not alarmingly so until the last few days. I wired G.P. to stand by, but the end came before he could get here. He arrives tomorrow morning from N.Y.

I had planned to go to Denver for the balloon races over the fourth as referee, but now, of course, those

plans will have to be cancelled. Dorothy will train back
to Tulsa. A sad ending for what has been a pleasant
visit.

In the meantime I'd like to hear an account of your
and Nancy's wanderings. So far nary a word has come.
Please send news by air mail as I'm busting to know
what you think of Merry England, etc, etc, etc.

Our house is coming along *slowly*. I am afraid you'll
have to live in a tent for a while under a cactus. I'll
have some word for you when you land.

Have a good time and dance with the Prince of
Wales.

Yr. doter,

A

On July 22, the Los Angeles *Times* devoted a wide part of its
front page to a picture of Amelia and her new flying laboratory,
similar to the United States airmail stamp that in 1963 com-
memorated her contribution to aviation. Wearing soft shoes or
moccasins, light slacks, a bunchy dark leather jacket, and a loosely
knotted silk scarf, Amelia looked still to be in her teens, with
her blue eyes direct into the camera and her light hair blown
by the wind. Behind her was the two-motored Lockheed Electra,
its identification number NR 16020 fairly visible on the under-
wing. Flying as copilot to Elmer C. McLeod, Lockheed's test flyer,
she had the day before given the plane its first official flight.

The accompanying news story described the $70,000 ship as
"equipped for a possible nonstop flight of 4500 miles," and enu-
merated such special equipment as "blind flying instruments, a
Sperry autogiro robot pilot, a fuel minimizer, wind de-icers, radio
homing and two-way sending devices." Extra fuel tanks were yet
to be mounted, three on each wing and six more in the fuselage.
"We've improved the mechanical features of aviation marvel-
lously," Amelia explained, "but the observation of the human
factor in flight has been neglected." She might, she went on,

discover that flying at 10,000 feet demanded a different diet from that served at sea level.

Two days later, on her thirty-ninth birthday, she took official delivery of the plane, and to President Edward C. Elliot and the Trustees of Purdue University she said, "My ambition is to have this wonderful gift produce practical results for the future of commercial flying and for the women who may want to fly tomorrow's planes." When she applied to the Department of Commerce in Los Angeles for a restricted aircraft license she wrote "Long distance flights and research" as the plane's designated use.

Life must have looked pretty swell to Amelia Mary Earhart Putnam that summer of 1936. She was in total control of her existence, her marriage was at least stable, and GP was really very good at raising funds and running such errands as meeting his mother-in-law on her return from Europe. Amelia had her new airplane to play with, and the plans for the next flight were well along. After that she intended no more long-distance flying. Literally there would be no more oceans to cross for the first time, and anyway she would tell Carl Allen of the New York *Herald Tribune* in a few months, "I'm getting old and want to make way for the new generation before I get feeble."

No one mentioned that the Lockheed Electra was named for the "lost" star of the Pleiades. If something should happen, however, that was as Amelia wanted it, to die with her plane doing the thing she most loved, flying alone into the silence of the sky.

TWENTY

First Takeoff
1936-1937

The round-the-world flight was the most daring yet proposed by any pilot, and since Amelia believed that the success of any long and dangerous flight depended in great part on careful preparation, she now began an intensive training program. To practice instrument flying, she spent hundreds of hours locked in a Link blind-flying trainer which Paul Mantz installed in his Burbank hangar, and she spent many more hours than usual in test flying the Electra before she and her advisers were satisfied with its performance. In addition to these preparations, she was busy campaigning for President Roosevelt's re-election, supervising alterations to the new house, lecturing, and shopping personally for trophies to be awarded to winners in the women's handicap event which she sponsored at the 1936 National Air Races.

She was so busy in California that GP was delegated to go to the pier in New York to meet Mrs. Earhart and Nancy Balis when they returned from Europe. Amelia talked to her mother by telephone and did not again write of the European trip.

Los Angeles, [August 23, 1936]

Dear Maw,

I have been so busy I haven't had time to write. Here are some more pix of the house. We moved the original as you can see and began from the beginning.

It will be nice I think eventually.
Writing later.

A

New York, [September 28, 1936]

Dear Mother,
    Home again — for a few days. We, GP and I will be in Boston Sat. and Sun. and will drop around to see you either Sat. eve or Sun. morn.
    We wanna talk with P and Albert. I'll let you know just when later. If Pidge wants me to know anything or bring out anything or suggest action, have her write me here.
    Here's small checkie.

A.

Muriel Morrissey had reached another crisis in her marriage, and talked once more of separation and divorce. In a letter to her mother in England early in the summer, she had not made much of her unhappiness, although it was obvious Mrs. Earhart's absence was hard on her. And perhaps it was in dismay that she heard Amelia and George announce their intention of setting aside a room in the new California house for Amy, a room GP thought "just about the swellest in the whole house," with a bathroom which was a "Roman dream of elegance."

Pidge could never begrudge her mother anything; she just couldn't bear the thought of trying to cope without her. As usual lack of money was the main problem, but on the visit to Medford, Amelia and George provided an advance to see the family through the current financial crisis. The Morrissey household, with Mrs. Earhart once more in residence, subsided into the fall routine of school, Halloween, Thanksgiving, and Christmas.

The Putnams spent the 1937 New Year holiday with Floyd and Jacqueline Cochran Odlum at their ranch in Indio, where Amelia was able to ride horseback or relax in the swimming pool or lie in the winter sunshine. A number of her friends, including Jacqueline, were not in favor of the equatorial flight. All of them had complete confidence in Amelia's professional ability and judgment; it was the long uncharted distances over water that they feared. The Electra was, after all, a land plane. Amelia listened and nodded and met all objections with a grin. She knew they were right, she knew there were risks, and despite all, she knew what she had to do. She had to make the flight. Nothing else mattered.

Because both women had in the past been interested in experimenting with extrasensory perception, however, Amelia could not entirely ignore Jacqueline's worries. Jacqueline had twice confirmed with Amelia facts or figures she could not otherwise have known, and now she had an uneasy feeling that Captain Manning, whom she admired enormously as the navigator of a seagoing vessel, was just not capable of high-speed celestial navigation in an airplane. At her friend's suggestion, Amelia took the captain some distance offshore, circled a few times, and asked him to chart the course back to Los Angeles. Manning was 200 miles off in his calculation.

In the end, Captain Frederick J. Noonan agreed to assist Captain Manning and to spell Amelia at the controls over the Pacific, at least as far as Howland Island. Noonan was a former Pan American Airways pilot and navigator who had sailed the seas from the age of seventeen until after World War I, when he switched to flying. He had been the inspector of all Pan American airports until he was detailed to map the new Far East Pacific routes for the company. Unfortunately he was an alcoholic, and Pan American had let him go as too great a risk, a circumstance Amelia ignored in favor of his unquestioned skill at celestial navigation and his fervent assurances that he was recovered from his drinking problem.

Early in January as expenses mounted, George went East to arrange more financing. His idea was to persuade the commercial airlines to contribute to the flight and capitalize on Amelia as their own best advertisement, and several agreed. His big achievement was an arrangement with Gimbels in New York to sell letter covers that Amelia would carry with her and, along the route, mail back to collectors. Printed in red and blue, decorated with stars, the white envelopes were distinctive, with a full-face photograph of Amelia and a logo of the world with an airplane whizzing around it. Ten thousand of them sold. George added more than $25,000 to the kitty, which already included royalties from Amelia's books and fees from her speaking engagements.

Still in California, Amelia lectured as usual and continued with her strenuous training and testing schedules. Late in the month she learned from Mrs. Earhart that trouble had flared again in West Medford, and on January 31 she typed a letter to her sister which she sent to George to read and mail from New York.

Los Angeles, January 31, 1937

Dear Muriel,

I am deeply sorry to hear further reports of your unhappy domestic situation. I had hoped that the money GPP and I advanced would help Albert grow up...

You have taken entirely too much on the chin for your own good or that of any man who holds the purse strings. I sometimes feel that adult human beings owe as much to themselves as to others, for by asserting individual rights, the baser natures of those who have them are held in check. That is often very hard to do. One hesitates to bring on a quarrel when it can be avoided by giving in. But perhaps one definite assertion will prevent the slow accumulation of a sense of superiority in a person who really should not claim superiority. Given a little power over another, little natures swell to hideous proportions. It is hopeless to watch a character change of this kind in one you have cared for — a few rows might have been less suffering in the long run.

What's done is done. The problem is what to do now. . . You will probably have to obtain a legal separation in order to get a monthly income. Please do not go to any old lawyer on this. I am coming east this week and unless events move too fast, hold the legal part until I get to NY. If you have to see someone, go to the man whose name I gave you before. And don't SIGN ANYTHING IN THE MEANTIME. Do not even write letters to Albert on the subject of divorce or separation. Don't move out of the house away from Albert no matter how tough things may get, until you see a lawyer. Keep me informed through letter or telegram (collect) what is happening. . .

You had better plan to come out here for the summer. Or before, if you have to. Something can be worked out. It is hard to give up the school just when it is beginning to pay but human crises have a way of happening at inconvenient times. Anyway living is cheaper and the fleebitten [sic] New England atmosphere far away. Then Albert *might* miss you and the children if you came. It's worth trying.

Ster
A.E.

Amelia now decided that Mrs. Earhart should move more or less permanently to North Hollywood, whatever the outcome should be in West Medford.

[Telegram from Burbank]
February 8, 1937

EXPECT LEAVE FOR NEWYORK TODAY WILL SEE MURIEL IN NEXT FEW DAYS OF COURSE COUNT ON ME FOR ANYTHING NECESSARY IN CRISES STOP SHE SHOULD SEE ATTORNEY IN MEANTIME IF SHE NO LONGER HAS ADDRESS MAN I REFERRED HER TO WIRE GP TO GET AGAIN THROUGH CHESTER MCLAUGHLIN IN NEW YORK STOP LEGAL SEPARATION

NECESSARY TO INSURE INCOME FOR CHILDREN SHE MAY
HAVE TO REMAIN IN BOSTON SOMETIME WHILE THIS
ARRANGED TELL HER UNDER NO CIRCUMSTANCES LEAVE
HOUSE BEFORE ALBERT DOES KEEP ME INFORMED THROUGH
GPP - A

[Telegram from Burbank]
February 23, 1937

ONE HUNDRED BERRIES BY CHECK TODAY TO GET YOU
SETTLED HOPE YOU CAN FIND DECENT ACCOMMODATIONS
THERE PLEASE DONT CONTRACT TO KEEP EITHER OF
CHILDREN AS I MIGHT NEED YOU SUDDENLY ANYWAY HOUSE
SHOULD BE FINISHED IN THREE WEEKS STOP SUGGEST YOU
SHIP ALL BELONGINGS NOT NEEDED JUST NOW HERE AS
PLANNED - AE

While family problems crowded her private thinking, Amelia,
in a dark blue wool dress with Captain Manning beside her,
appeared at the Barclay hotel in New York for a press conference
her husband had set up. As the newsreel cameras whirred and
photoflashes lit the room, she made her announcement of the
world trip, and traced the route on a large wall map. Paul Mantz,
she said, would go with the plane as far as Honolulu; Captain
Noonan would aid Captain Manning with the navigation, and
depending on weather conditions ahead, Amelia hoped to leave
both navigators in Australia, or possibly Brazil, and complete
the flight alone.

The newspapers exploded with the story: BOSTONIAN WILL
BE FIRST WOMAN TO FLY AROUND THE GLOBE, the Sunday
Boston *Globe* reported, devoting a page of its rotogravure
section to a map of Amelia's route, a photograph of the plane,
and a picture of Amelia as a school girl. "What flight of imagination was she having then?" the caption asked; and another picture
showed her being mobbed in Southampton in 1928. The paper
also announced it had secured exclusive rights to print the Earhart

story, although later Amelia's columns were syndicated by the New York *Herald Tribune.*

Various contradictions appeared from then on in many papers, such as the story in the Los Angeles *Times* stating that "Only Capt. Manning will accompany her when she soars westward from Oakland. He will leave the Lockheed at Darwin, Australia. 'From that point on, I'll go it alone,' said Miss Earhart. 'Probably I'll wish I had Capt. Manning with me before I get back home!' "

As the middle of March approached, and Amelia was prevented by heavy rains even from setting a tentative departure date from Oakland, George promptly nominated Los Angeles, which had never even been considered, as a reasonable alternate. "Fully loaded, Miss Earhart's plane could take off from any of the five runways at Union Air Terminal," he said, and added that Captain Manning had assured Miss Earhart that "a new course departing from Los Angeles could be plotted to Hawaii in a few minutes." He was making news out of what was no more than a minor weather delay.

Amelia went along with the publicity, issuing statements through her husband and avoiding the reporters whenever she could. Once she took the Electra up for a forty-five-minute test flight out over the Golden Gate to check the compass and radio equipment, and later the same day she took off again with Manning, Mantz, and Noonan aboard. Everyone thought she was on her way. Two hours later she was back at the Oakland Airport, where George told reporters it was just another test flight, and added that "it had not been decided whether Noonan would accompany Miss Earhart and her navigator..." when he knew perfectly well the matter had been settled for weeks.

On the 17th, two Pan American Clippers finally took off from Oakland. When the rain ceased about 4:30 P.M., Amelia's plane was brought out of the Navy hangar, and Paul Mantz ran engine checks. With no formal announcement, he taxied the transport to the head of the 7000-foot runway the airport authorities had constructed especially for the Electra. Shortly Amelia arrived in a Navy car and, waving goodbye to George, slid into the pilot's seat as Mantz moved over to her right. Manning and Noonan were already in their places at the chart table, which was bolted down in the cabin. Amelia revved the engines, and on signal from the control tower the Electra started down the runway, the five-ton ship gathering speed and lifting off in less than 3000 feet, with 4000 to spare.

A departure no one was prepared for, except a San Francisco *Chronicle* photographer to whom someone leaked the news. Circling in a rented plane over San Francisco Bay, he finally caught the Electra as it passed over the Golden Gate Bridge, capturing forever not only a beautiful picture but a moment in history.

Amelia and her crew landed 15 hours and 52 minutes later at Wheeler Field in Honolulu, setting a record for the east to west crossing. They had encountered absolutely nothing of note en route from the mainland.

An auspicious beginning with jubilation for everyone. Paul's fiancée, Terry Minor, was there, together with Chris and Mona Holmes, at whose Waikiki house Amelia and George had stayed in 1935. When a storm delayed for a day the start of the second lap, the genial couple invited friends to come for a luau and meet their distinguished guest. But Amelia walked away from the party, striding far down the beach beneath Diamond Head, a slim and lonely figure in the same brown slacks and leather jacket she had worn from Oakland. She was nearly forty years old and looked younger.

She was, or seemed to be, everywhere at ease, although casual acquaintances said she was remote and aloof. Other people found her always courteous, if often preoccupied and sometimes dull. Although her intellectuality was not profound, her intelligence and knowledge were prodigious. Next to wanting to fly, her greatest desire was probably for privacy, the right to be solitary or sociable as *she* chose, not as the public wanted her wherever she went and was recognized. She had become adroit at evading social commitments with strangers or casual acquaintances by professing to have a "date to go ground flying" with some pilot friends. In time her mother would write, "[Amelia] liked people and enjoyed the contact with other minds, but . . . she didn't enjoy arguing, perhaps because she had well thought out plans or if she hadn't yet made her decisions . . . there was greater reason for saying nothing until she had marshalled her facts. If she was puzzled that was entirely different and she was inclined to try her ideas on others."

One can guess how impatient she must have been at that moment in Honolulu, how resentful of the storm that delayed takeoff for Howland Island, and how extremely fatigued from the long months of grueling preparations, the many test flights, the lecture schedules and travel, and the family demands and concerns. She might even be as "groggy" now as Paul Mantz had called her the day before when she needed him to take over the controls and land the Electra.

The plane had been moved to Luke Field near Pearl Harbor, where it was refueled, and Amelia had rested during the day, sleeping and swimming in the sunshine she loved. She was ready to take off this very minute, to get away on this final adventure which would give her a rest from reporters and fans, and from the family and its problems. Also from GP and his strenuous energy, which sometimes taxed her strength.

In *Last Flight*, Amelia wrote of George that he felt "grim satisfaction — a species of modern martyrdom — in being, for once, the male left behind while the female fares forth adventure-bound, thus turning topsy-turvy the accepted way of the world in such matters." Now possibly she wondered what the future would be like for them and their marriage. "It *is* hard to be old," she once had said. "I'm afraid I'd hate it." Moreover, commercial aviation was establishing regular schedules in so many directions that little opportunity remained for dangerous and lonely "first" flights by anyone. This would be her last, and then she would settle into a routine existence of some kind, perhaps aviation research, or counseling young women. She would have time for books, friends, leisurely travel, her home in North Hollywood, and all that good California sunshine. She would have George and her marriage. For all the rest of her years.

Amelia turned back to the party on the beach, said a few polite words to her hosts and their guests, and went to bed. She rose again long before dawn, dressed quickly, and with Manning and Noonan went out to Luke Field. Paul Mantz was already there, checking the engines and visually examining every inch of the Electra. He put a lei of paper orchids around Amelia's neck, and watched anxiously as she followed her two navigators into the plane. Then the door closed, and Mantz stood back, joining nearly a hundred Army officers who had gathered in the dawn to watch the takeoff.

With Manning at the chart table in the cabin and Noonan in the copilot's seat beside her, Amelia started the engines, and when she was satisfied with their sound and performance, she signaled the ground crew to remove the wheel chocks.

The plane moved sluggishly along the wet runway, until, as Amelia told it later, "... Suddenly the plane pulled to my right. I reduced the power on the opposite engine and succeeded in swinging from the right to the left. For a moment I thought I would be able to gain control and straighten the course. But, alas, the load was so heavy, once it started an arc there was nothing to do but let the plane ground loop as easily as possible... the landing gear on the right was wrenched free and gasoline sprayed from the drain-well..."

May Day!

Because Amelia kept her head and cut the ignition, there was neither an explosion nor a fire.

Paul Mantz hitched a ride as ambulances and fire trucks went screaming along the runway, and he was among the first to reach the crash. Already a deathly pale Amelia had hauled herself out and jumped to the ground after Manning and Noonan. None of them was hurt, all three were shaken.

"Something must have gone wrong," Amelia said, staring down

at the wreckage of one wing. "I don't know what happened, Paul."

A controversy arose as to what had actually caused the crash. The Boston *Evening American* reported that "the plane skidded on the wet concrete runway when the right tire blew out, wrecking the undercarriage." Other reports said Amelia simply lost control, or that the gasoline was unevenly loaded, or that she had "jock-eyed the throttle," a theory of Paul's which Amelia did not accept. Although she never came to a definite conclusion for herself, she believed a shock absorber might have given way.

Of one thing there was no doubt. Amelia was determined to take off again as soon as the plane could be returned to the Lockheed factory in Burbank and repaired. "Of course the flight is still on," she told reporters. "Of course I'll be back. I want to try it again." When someone said, "I understand your husband is greatly relieved because you can't go on with the flight," Amelia answered, "I know better. Just to put Mr. Putnam's attitude correctly into the record, here is what he wired me after learning he still had a wife to wire to: 'So long as you and the boys are OK, the rest doesn't matter. After all blown tire is just one of those things. Whether you want to call it a day or keep going later is equally jake with me.' "

Within hours, Amelia had telephoned George in Oakland about the arrangement for the plane to be shipped to Los Angeles, and consigned the 10,000 plus letter covers, which were recovered from the wreck, to the United States postal authorities in Honolulu for safekeeping until further instructions. Then, looking very white and tired, she and the three men boarded the *Malolo*, which sailed for Los Angeles at noon.

TWENTY-ONE

Second Takeoff
1937

At seventy Amy Otis Earhart was erect, white-haired, and energetic, as much given to rapid walking as to writing long letters to family, friends, and fans of her famous daughter. She saved all those she received, too; in fact, she rarely threw anything away. Letters, telegrams, greeting cards, newspaper clippings, recipes, package wrappings, pins and needles and thread and string, Amy saved them all. "Waste not, want not," she would murmur when challenged, "that's what Grandmother Harres used to say."

She wore a hearing device in her left ear and needed glasses for close work, but quickly took them off when she was meeting strangers or being photographed. When traveling, she liked a tailored suit, a shirtwaist and tie, or occasionally a lacy jabot, and she rarely left home without gloves and a hat. Always she walked in sturdy oxfords, neatly laced and securely tied over ankles that tended to swell slightly. Considering her years and the many household tasks she got through every day she was in excellent health. She doted on giving to or doing for those she loved or befriended, women and children mostly, and deferred as a totally dependent gentlewoman should to the superiority of men. It is extremely unlikely that she thought of herself as unfulfilled, and she would vigorously have denied any suggestion that she was archetypal. Anyone who ever met her loved her at once and for as long as he or she lived.

In her own way Amy was always prepared for the telephone call which came to West Medford about eleven in the morning of March 20. At news of Amelia's plane crash in Honolulu she sat down suddenly, grabbing an old envelope and jotting notes as she listened: "Take of [sic] at sunrise...plane 100 yards down runway burst into flames. Plane in full speed at time...Miss Earhart escaped plane damaged tire blows out...Amelia is all right going to continue flight..." Naturally Amy wouldn't rest until she saw her daughter safe and well again. Whenever Amelia prepared to go anywhere, or said goodbye, or didn't appear or telephone as expected, concern inevitably struck deep at her mother. This time she was all right, and Mrs. Earhart gave thanks.

"I might need you suddenly," Amelia had telegraphed a month ago. It was a long time since AE had really needed anyone, and Amy was pleased, although how it would be living with Amelia and George, she couldn't judge. She always enjoyed visiting in California, where the excitement of Amelia's life contrasted so markedly with Muriel's. The coming and going, the telephone ringing off the hook, and the great bags of mail delivered daily to the house. She had her own circle in Los Angeles, and Amelia's friends were always most cordial and loving to her as well. The Ninety-Nines had practically adopted her: they sent cards and flowers to her on holidays and never forgot her birthday.

This year Muriel and the two children were coming after school closed, and when Amelia's flight was over the three Earhart women would be together again as in the good days past. Perhaps GP would have business in New York or take a trip somewhere. He never rested long in any one place.

Before the day ended, Amy learned that Amelia was already aboard the *Malolo*, and later, by reading the Boston *Globe* she followed her daughter's plans for the second world takeoff. "This morning," Amelia wrote on March 26, "I completed my fourth voyage between Hawaii and the mainland...This last return was not intended when I took off a week ago..."

Since Amelia never talked much about her emotions, Amy

had to imagine how her daughter felt as she watched the Electra lowered over the side of the ship that brought it back from Hawaii. As she would later write, ". . .[Amelia and I] considered the plane she used as if it were a living creature. It was like a favorite pony. We said goodnight to it and petted its nose and almost fed it apples. The last plane. . .was the one we were especially attached to. . ."

After engineers at the Burbank Lockheed factory examined and tested the Electra for a week, Amelia reported that it would require a minimum of five weeks and $25,000 to replace the damaged parts and do some redesigning to accommodate the weight of extra equipment and fuel. She added that "Despite these troubles, there seem to me many reasons for trying to complete the flight. . .I would rather be a pilot on such an inspiring air voyage than on any I could imagine in the present state of adventuring. . ."

Because of seasonal weather patterns, takeoff was tentatively scheduled for the end of May, and the route was reversed. Amelia would fly from Oakland via Miami to South America, across Africa and down to Australia. From there to New Guinea, and then the long and dangerous leg over the uncharted south-central Pacific to Howland Island, followed by Honolulu and home to Oakland.

First there was $50,000 to raise, however. The twenty-five for Lockheed to repair the plane, and another twenty-five to rearrange flight authorizations and reposition caches of fuel and spare parts along the reversed route. As Amelia said more than once, "I am more or less mortgaging my future to go on. But what are futures for?"

George obligingly went East and arranged a second agreement with Gimbels. Another set of letter covers was printed, identical to the first except for the addition of "2nd TAKE OFF" in a red box placed beneath Amelia's picture and the logo of the world with the airplane circling it. Many of those who had bought the first covers now rushed to purchase the second issue and assure themselves of a unique postal commemorative.

Amelia reluctantly let a few devoted friends know how in need she was, and among those who responded was Bernard Baruch, who sent her $2500 because he liked her "everlasting guts." Admiral Byrd sent a check for $1500, reminding her of the 1928 cigarette advertisement and the fee in the same amount that she donated to his Antarctic expedition because she didn't smoke. Floyd and Jacqueline Cochran Odlum advanced a substantial sum, and the mechanics at the Lockheed plant worked an entire Sunday to meet the repair deadline and refused to accept pay for it.

In mid-April Amelia went East on business and then to Medford to see the Morrissey family and fly Mrs. Earhart to California. The sisters talked over Muriel's marital problems, and as she had in her January letter Amelia advised Pidge she must absolutely establish a satisfactory property and support agreement before leaving her husband and the family home. Once this was done, she could come on to California with the children for the summer and look for a teaching job in North Hollywood. Amelia and Amy flew off to Burbank believing the plans were definite.

Amy, an enthusiastic air traveler, enjoyed the flight to California and, most of all, the arrival at the new house in North Hollywood. Sited on two lots beside the Toluca Lake golf course, it was spacious and tastefully furnished. After his mother's death the previous summer, George had brought some of her things from Connecticut, including a lovely old desk that he later gave to Mrs. Earhart. Other furniture, including Amelia's carved teakwood trophy chest, had come from Rye.

Beside the usual family rooms in the original house, a large addition incorporated a study both Putnams used, and the master bedroom, guest rooms, and staff quarters. In a corner with a view over the golf course to the Hollywood hills was Mrs. Earhart's room. She liked it at once and happily recognized a small walnut table from her girlhood home in Atchison. On it was a new globe of the world, illuminated from inside, so she could follow Amelia's flight around the Equator.

A Filipino houseman, Fred, was responsible for inside heavy chores and maintenance, and for washing and polishing Amelia's 1936 Cord 8 Phaeton convertible sedan. Outside and out of sight, he cultivated a vegetable garden for the family table, and tended the palm trees, mesquite, agaves and other gigantic succulents, including a century plant due to bloom on or near Amelia's July birthday.

Margot DeCarie, an emotional and adventurous young woman who had been a persistent fan before Amelia employed her as a Girl Friday, lived in and held herself responsible for household accounts, fan letters, files, photographs, and any other chore she could devise for her adored Miss Earhart. In 1941, her love and loyalty already transferred to Mrs. Earhart, Margot joined a search for the lost Electra, but because of World War II, the ship never departed from Honolulu.

Josephine "Joe" Berger Greer frequently came from New York, where for years she was the devoted secretary for both Putnams, although technically employed by George. Much later, she and her husband Win moved into a residence only a few blocks from the Putnam Hollywood house, and together they accompanied George on his photographic expedition to Central America on the yacht *Athene* late in 1937. Joe also adored Mrs. Earhart.

Amy fitted easily into the lively household and took much joy in watching Amelia at home. Behind the public person who seemed so remote and unfamiliar in the newspapers, Amelia was still her beloved firstborn. She would lie flat on her stomach in the living room to read an article, or toss a salad to go with whatever George, who loved to cook, had concocted for dinner on cook's day out, or lick the bowl with her finger when Amy iced a chocolate cake.

With new people to meet, new walks to take, and all the news that filled her letters to family and friends, Amy was carefree, except for her continuing concern about Pidge's unhappiness. Once again Muriel had changed her mind. She wrote that after all she was not leaving Albert to come to California. The security of a home and father seemed to her more important for her children than any material benefits they would receive through Amelia's influence and efforts. As for herself, joy in her children and giving them a full and happy life was worth the price.

The decision worried Amy and annoyed Amelia extremely. Both had tried long and hard to help Muriel, and Amelia greatly resented the fact that her advice and opinion had so little effect on her sister. Yet she agreed with Amy that Muriel not only had her own reasons for staying with Albert but in the end the decision was really hers alone to make.

Eventually Muriel took satisfaction in completing her education and becoming a successful and beloved high school teacher in Medford. Whatever the truth of her marriage, she and Albert were known as a happy couple, thanks to Muriel's pride and her need to maintain appearances in her chosen social surroundings. Later, she became the main source of private information about the Earhart family and its most illustrious member, and was the devoted keeper of her sister's private and public image.

In 1937, however, Amelia had little time to spend discussing Muriel's problems with their mother. She was far too busy, too involved in the incredibly complex preparations and strenuous training required for this, the last and most important flight of her career. Practical arrangements were almost complete, the money was in the bank or had been paid out, and the Electra was nearly ready to fly. Captain Manning had long ago returned to his ship, and the newly married Captain Noonan was in Oakland with his bride, awaiting the second takeoff. When the flight was over he planned to open a school for aerial navigators, and although George had forbidden his using Amelia's name or his part in the flight to advertise it, Fred had her permission to go ahead. She even promised to help him in the venture.

Only Paul Mantz and George Putnam were unhappy, Paul because he thought Amelia listened more to her husband than was wise and GP because he thought she didn't listen enough. She had decided several matters against his wishes, not only advertising the school but keeping Noonan with her all the way, for example. George had pointed out that her flying solo, at least on the last leg of the flight, would add luster to the AE legend and greatly increase publicity about the adventure as it progressed. Amelia was adamant. She needed navigational help, and she decreed no part of the way alone and no public announcement of departure until after she and Noonan were already in the air out of Miami and were committed.

As she later wrote in the Miami *Herald*, "So much was written before and after the March takeoff at Oakland, and following the Honolulu accident, that I thought it would be a pleasant change just to slip away without comment. . . If one gives out plans beforehand, one is likely to be charged with publicity seeking by those who do not know how difficult it is to escape the competent gentlemen of the press. On the other hand, if one slips away as I have generally tried to do, the slipper-away invites cat calls from those who earn their living writing and taking photographs. . ."

Paul Mantz was still dissatisfied with the radio equipment and believed it needed more tests or even partial replacement. He also felt George was pushing Amelia too fast and too far, and was too influential in the decisions Amelia made. He was both frightened and furious when he learned about the removal of the 250-foot trailing radio antenna he had ordered to be installed. When he wrote to Amelia protesting, and urging its reinstallation, George answered that the technicians had the radio problem licked without it.

Actually, the perhaps fatal decision to remove the antenna was Amelia's own, because reeling it out and back struck her as an unnecessary annoyance. Its absence, however, would create a long time period in the south-central Pacific when the Electra would be totally out of touch with ground stations and any ships at sea, including: the USS *Ontario*, on station halfway between Lae, New Guinea, and Howland Island, 2556 miles apart; the Coast Guard Cutter *Itasca*, standing off the island; and the USS *Swan*, lying halfway between Howland and Hawaii. And if Amelia's signals were so weak nobody could hear her, neither could she receive signals from anyone. Safe completion of this most dangerous leg of the flight was going to depend entirely on Fred Noonan's navigational skill and accuracy.

The not always pacific waters were vast and the island was only a tiny dot on Amy Earhart's illuminated globe. Without her glasses she couldn't even see it when Amelia described the whole route one day. Nor did she listen too closely to what Amelia said of the treeless island, only a mile square, with a maximum elevation of twenty feet, or of compass bearings and when to change headings. But she clearly understood that if Amelia and Fred made it to Howland, the rest of the flight would be easy. Comparatively speaking.

Discovered by American traders in 1842 and claimed in 1857, the island had no landing facilities for an airplane, and was in fact almost totally undeveloped. When Amelia asked the Department of the Interior for permission to refuel there, she was refused because of a tight budget. Army Air Corps friends then urged her to appeal to the President. After consulting with his military advisers, Roosevelt was delighted to oblige. He authorized government funds for the construction of a primitive airfield with three runways, not out of friendship alone but to establish an advance airbase close to the Mandated Islands. Administered by Germany before World War I, the Marianas, Carolines, and Marshalls had been fortified in defiance of the League of Nations mandate and were closed to non-Japanese without exception. Yet they lay widely spread across the sea lanes and prospective air routes from Hawaii to the Philippines and East Indies, thus constituting a serious threat to United States security in the Pacific.

Old Asia Hands who believed war with Japan was inevitable and considered these islands the key to victory or defeat included General Billy Mitchell of the United States Army Air Corps, who circled the boundaries of the proscribed area in 1923 and predicted a Sunday morning attack on Pearl Harbor. His advocacy of a large air force independent of the army led to his court-martial

in 1926, and not until after World War II was his recommenda-
tion accepted. In 1921 Lieutenant Colonel Earl ("Pete") Ellis of
the United States Marine Corps also had predicted a Japanese
attack on the Hawaiian Islands, and in 1923 he had penetrated
the Marshalls and Carolines as a German trader, was discovered
and murdered there. Any further attempt to assess the strength
of Japanese forces in the Mandated Islands simply could not be
made.

By 1937 the certainty of the military community that war was
inevitable between the United States and Japan was not shared
by Congress, which maintained an isolationist position, along
with most of the public, who had not yet heard of Yap or Truk,
of Kwajalein or Saipan along the bloody way to Iwo Jima. Official snooping in the forbidden area was impossible, even courtesy
calls by the United States Navy were refused; but a private venture
fairly nearby was discreetly to be given all possible aid.

A few people later believed, and some still do, that Amelia's
flight plan along the Equator was charted to include a secret di-
rective personally from President Roosevelt to overfly and possibly to photograph the Mandated Islands, despite the increased
distance and greater hazards. Muriel Earhart Morrissey in *Courage
Is the Price* said, however, "I am certain that he [President Roose-
velt] would not have expected Amelia to make the large-scale
detour necessary to fly over any Japanese-held territory." Mrs.
Roosevelt later assured Amelia's sister in writing that the President had never spoken to her of such a mission, nor had Amelia.
Furthermore, no evidence was ever found in the writings of either.

Along the same line was the insistence of some believers that
Amelia and Fred were victims of a tragically mismanaged "disappearance," staged to allow the Navy to conduct a wide sea
search, and that unfortunately, she and Noonan were actually
captured and either died naturally, or were executed by the
Japanese on Saipan. No government or military official, no
civilian, no one anywhere at any time ever admitted the truth
of this speculation, nor of many others which multiplied during

and after World War II and still make news from time to time.

Only Mrs. Earhart, years later, would say, "Amelia told me many things, but there were some things she couldn't tell me. I am convinced she was on some sort of government mission, possibly on verbal orders." No evidence to prove this statement has ever been found.

On May 17 Lockheed announced the Electra was ready to go, and Amelia tested it the next day. On the 19th, with George and her mechanic Bo McKneely as passengers, she flew to Oakland to pick up Captain Noonan. The following day the second attempt to fly around the world at the Equator began when, officially but in secret, Amelia "just slipped away without comment..."

The Los Angeles *Times* reported later that her Oakland take-off was designed to give the plane a shakedown following the recent repairs; and, after describing a small fire in the left motor which caused an overnight delay in Tucson, added that George left the plane in New Orleans to take a train for New York. Amelia and Fred continued to Miami, where they arrived on May 23. To reporters who met her at the Municipal Airport, Amelia said, "The party will return to California after repairs [to the radio] are completed."

During the following nine days, while Bo McKneely and the Pan American mechanics and radio technicians worked on the Electra, Amelia spent most of her time at the airport. Sometimes she ground-tested the instruments, and sometimes she flew the ship to check out its performance. As always her main concern was to prepare as expertly and as completely as possible for every contingency that could be anticipated. She never hinted at impatience, and often got as filthy with grease as the men working on the plane, because she worked along with them. As Fred Noonan wrote to his bride, "She is an excellent pilot and is willing to work like a grease monkey when necessary." She was also willing to cross the highway from the airport and eat lunch with the men at a "greasy spoon."

After GP and his son David joined her, Amelia took a day off to go fishing for pompano, which she had grown to like, but they had no luck. Another day, she and Fred visited the chief mechanic for Pan American, W. G. Richards, who conducted them over the airline's international air terminal and maintenance base at Dinner Key. While Amelia surveyed and evaluated the efficiency of the hangar-workshops where the company's Sikorsky Clipper ships were periodically inspected and overhauled, Fred renewed acquaintance with many men whom he had met when he was manager of the Pan Am Airport at Port au Prince, Haiti.

On Tuesday, June 1, 1937, just before 6:00 A.M., with only her husband and stepson David, Bo McKneely, and Miami airport personnel looking on, Amelia Earhart and Fred Noonan climbed into the Electra and lifted off for San Juan, Puerto Rico, on the first officially recorded leg of the round-the-world flight. When they were 100 miles out, a Miami radio station broke into a program to alert the public, and for the next thirty-two days major stories of the flight appeared regularly on the front pages of the world's newspapers.

Every day in North Hollywood, Amy Earhart clipped the articles and the syndicated daily columns Amelia sent back to the New York *Herald Tribune*, and every day in black ink she traced each segment of the flight on the illuminated globe of the world. Sometimes she took out and reread an unsigned and undated note in Amelia's handwriting:

> *Very confidentially* I may hop off in a few days. I am going to try to beat the newspapers. So you don't know nothin'.
>
> While I am gone you will probably need a cool dress or two. Try Robinson's or Bullock's or Bullock's-Wilshire. I have accounts both places. Go early of a morning.
>
> Herewith some doe.

Or she may have read again what was almost certainly her last letter from Amelia:

> Miami, Florida
> June 1, 1937
>
> Hope to take off tomorrow A.M. to San Juan, Puerto Rico. Here is three hundred bucks for Margot to put in household fund.
>
> A

TWENTY-TWO

Lost Star
1937

On Friday, July 2, in the house on Valley Spring Lane, Margot DeCarie worked in the study after breakfast, Fred was busy gardening, and Mrs. Earhart was in her room reading the Los Angeles *Times* as she did the first thing every morning. Today Amelia and Captain Noonan were flying from Lae, New Guinea, to Howland, or perhaps they had already arrived at the tiny island. The international date line made it difficult to be certain: the Coast Guard wireless station in San Francisco reported intercepting a message to the cutter *Itasca*, waiting off Howland Island, in which Amelia indicated she would not take off from Lae until "tomorrow." Only it had been July 2, on New Guinea when she sent the message.

Also from the *Itasca* came an Associated Press story saying that American sailors and Coast Guardsmen were watching along one of the loneliest stretches of the earth's surface to guide Amelia Earhart on the longest and most hazardous flight of her career. Earlier articles had described the preparations for a possible crash landing: beach and offshore patrols, and a radio-telephone connection from the ship to the island, while work crews stood by prepared to shoot at huge flocks of native terns, frigate, and gooney birds (albatrosses) to drive them from the runway when the Electra approached touchdown.

Mrs. Earhart clipped both articles and started the black line from New Guinea toward Howland Island on her globe. Then she wrote a long letter and enclosed a bit of money for Muriel. Finished, she wrote a thank you note to Henry S. Linam of Caripito, a small town in the Venezuelan jungle where Amelia and Fred had landed just thirty days ago. Mr. Linam had written to tell her of the "honor and pleasure of knowing your famous daughter," and how Amelia wanted to send something typical from Venezuela, so along with photographs of her visit, he had mailed a luncheon set made from the moriche palm. The Indians, he said, pulled the fibers from the leaves, dampened and rolled them, and later wove them all by hand. Amy couldn't wait for the set to arrive. So loving of Amelia, and so kind of Mr. Linam to take all that trouble.

Again finished, she thumbed through the clippings relating to the flight. Someone was always sending her one more, and in thirty days a good many had accumulated. Eventually Margot or someone would paste them in the thick scrapbooks filled with all the AE stories dating back to 1928. Still there would be duplicates left over. Naturally Amy liked best those articles Amelia wrote herself, beginning with the departure from Miami, the overnight in San Juan, Puerto Rico, and then on to the jungle of Venezuela. They were syndicated by the New York *Herald Tribune,* and after Amelia returned home, she intended to put them all together for a book.

After Caripito, Amelia and Fred had flown to Paramaribo and Fort Aleza, Brazil, which Amelia had been "very glad to see sitting just where it should be. . ." From there, on to Natal and across the South Atlantic to St. Louis on the west coast of Africa. Amelia wrote expressively and put in many details, what she noticed about the terrain they flew over, and what impressed her about the people when they landed. Once she said that "Everywhere we go, someone steps up to offer food and shelter, baths and launderings."

On the far side of Africa she wrote that of course the Red Sea was blue from the air, and that she had never seen a more desolate section than the Arabian shore: low sandhills reaching almost to the water's edge and ragged mountains towering above, and no habitation except a few villages. Since she and Fred had come from a yellow fever district, she was getting used to being fumigated every time the plane landed and attendants rushed out with "flit guns" and began shooting.

Jacques de Sibour, a pilot and old friend, met them at Karachi. He gave Amelia maps she would need and assurances that all the supplies of fuel and extra parts he had arranged for were cached along the route ahead. During the two-day layover, while the plane was being tuned by Imperial Airway ground crews, Amelia mounted a camel for an excursion with Noonan and Sibour to an oasis outside the city. On the second day, she telephoned the *Herald Tribune* office in New York where, as prearranged, GP was waiting.

The conversation was recorded, and among other things Amelia told her husband she felt "Swell! Never better!" After details of the flight so far, she added, "Oh, yes, tell the stamp collectors that all the covers I'm carrying for them have got thus far safely. I expect to have 'em stamped and postmarked here or at Darwin or Lae..."

For a moment, the pair spoke off the record, and then it was "Goodbye...See you in Oakland." This final voice-to-voice contact between husband and wife had traveled 8274 miles from Karachi to Bombay to London by land lines, and across the North Atlantic by wireless telephone. Amelia and Fred were literally on the opposite side of the world from home.

After saying goodbye to Sibour in Karachi, Amelia flew over a sandstorm in the Sind Desert, and ran into an almost unbroken wall of water between Calcutta and Akyab, Burma, which proved to be the worst leg of the trip so far. The rain would have "drowned us if our cockpit hadn't been secure." Twice in an attempt to reach Bangkok, the monsoon forced a return to Akyab.

Then once again they took off, and from Rangoon Amelia wrote, "We let down and the bright grain plain beside the Irrawaddy River smiled up at us. Then we dodged about for fifty miles amid rain squalls...The first sight of Rangoon was the reflection of the sun touching a golden pagoda. This great structure stands on a rise of ground and could be seen for miles, while the city was still but a shadow on the horizon. Shortly after landing, rain poured down so heavily that it was hazardous to take off for Bangkok. It still is raining as I write."

The flyers stayed over with American Consul Austin Brady, who took them to visit the Golden Pagoda. "To enter," Amelia wrote, "one must be unshod and plod up long flights of steps, worn by numberless feet before. For the first time on the trip, Fred Noonan failed me. He would not take off his shoes and socks and go inside with me. He missed the sight of hundreds of Buddhas of all sizes in little stalls where drums and gongs are sold. Devotees were kneeling on mats and offering flowers before shrines, with sing-song prayers and strange jeweled ornaments..." The column ended with Amelia's hope of making Singapore the next day, providing the weather permitted.

The weather did. After refueling at Bangkok, she and Fred pushed on through clear skies that lasted down the Malay Archipelago clear to Bandoeng, Java, in the Dutch East Indies, now the Netherlands Indies. There Dutch Air Force and KLM technicians corrected a malfunctioning long-range navigational instrument. After the Electra took off for Darwin, the instrument failed again and forced a return to Bandoeng. The technicians then recommended a complete overhaul for the Electra.

Amelia and Fred finally arrived at Darwin, Australia, on June 27, and three days later she concluded an article from Lae, New Guinea, with the hope of soon rolling down the runway bound for points east, meaning Howland, Honolulu, and home for the Fourth of July...

Mrs. Earhart put the clippings away and prepared to answer a dozen neglected letters; after Amelia's return in the next few days there would be no time for correspondence.

At day's end, she sat down as usual to listen to the ten o'clock news over the radio. The Richfield reporter described Amelia's takeoff from Lae as "a thrilling one, with the large plane getting into the air with only fifty yards of runway to spare. Even now her huge plane is roaring over the South Pacific —"

Then the telephone rang.

It was George calling from San Francisco where he was keeping radio vigil at the Coast Guard wireless station.

Amy Earhart needed no headlines in the newspaper to imprint on her brain what her son-in-law told her. Yet next morning she couldn't avoid them: EARHART PLANE DOWN...AMELIA LOST IN PACIFIC...AE MISSES ISLAND ON LONG HOP...LADY LINDY LOST...

The Coast Guard was already searching, and the Navy was on the way, and they or someone in a small boat, perhaps a fishing boat, or on an isolated island or an atoll or coral reef, someone, surely someone would soon find Amelia and Fred. The dread that made Amy's heart pound and her breathing difficult would abate, and GP's fearful words about Amelia's failing to arrive at Howland Island would stop drumming in her ears — when Amelia was found.

Reporters were at the front door. As Margot DeCarie tried to take charge, Mrs. Earhart met them with dignity. They asked if she thought Amelia was dead. "No, no, no! No, of course not. I know she's all right. I know she will soon be found. I know she is alive." Then Margot reported that the rubber boat in the Electra was unseaworthy because she had tried it out herself right there in Toluca Lake. By then Mrs. Earhart was safely inside with the front door closed again.

Next day the news was more detailed. On the *Itasca*, lying off Howland Island, the radio watch had picked up the first contact with Amelia at 2:45 A.M. when they heard her calm voice through heavy static reporting "cloudy and overcast." The last time they heard her, at 8:45 A.M., she sounded anxious, her voice was urgent. "We are on a line of position 157 dash 337. Will repeat this message on 6210 kilocycles. We are running north and south." Her voice was not heard again on any radio frequency. Even though several messages indicated her belief that she had reached the island and was circling it, no one had secured a bearing on the plane. By noon of July 2, the Electra was presumed out of fuel and down.

On July 4, the Makapu Pan American Airways radio station, and the Coast Guard and Navy stations in Hawaii, combined to listen for a distinctive response to a radio message from KGMB in Honolulu, asking Amelia to signal if she heard the broadcast. Those listening all reported they heard the desired response. Later other radio stations and many ham operators also reported hearing those or similar signals from the plane.

When the *Itasca* sighted green flares northeast of Howland Island, the word went out: EARHART FOUND. But Paul Mantz killed the headline by reporting that Amelia had no flares aboard the Electra, and astronomers announced a shower of meteors.

As soon as he could get to Los Angeles, GP hurried to the Odlum apartment. Jacqueline Cochran told him where Amelia's plane was floating in the water, that Fred Noonan had a fractured skull and was unconscious, and Amelia was alive. She named the *Itasca*, of which she had never heard, and a Japanese fishing vessel nearby. When George relayed to the searchers where to look, nothing was found.

The Navy, on direct orders from President Roosevelt to Admiral William D. Leahy, sent the aircraft carrier *Lexington* with 300 Naval aviators aboard, the battleship *Colorado*, four destroyers, and a minesweeper to search over 250,000 square miles of Pacific Ocean, at an estimated cost of $4,000,000. And the world watched and hoped.

At first, in the middle of already multiplying contradictions, speculations, and rumors, Mrs. Earhart kept busy coping with her own emotions and sustaining family and friends with her invincible display of courage and good faith. Amelia and Fred would be found. No other circumstance was to be mentioned. Or thought about. By anyone. As the days passed, she responded personally to the many hundreds of sympathy messages arriving by mail from all over the world, some addressed only to "Mother of Amelia Earhart, California, U.S.A."

Muriel had telegraphed at once that she and her family were standing by, and other relatives and close friends communicated by telegram and letter. Tootie Challiss wrote, "How darling of *you* to write *me*...Nobody has to tell you how to stand things, Amelia gets her courage from you...GP says you are wonderful...and your fortitude has been an inspiration to him..."

A young woman said she had never written a letter "like this before, but I saw your daughter when she returned from her *Friendship* adventure in 1928. She looked like a glorious bird in her white costume with the white feather cloche on her head. I never asked for her autograph, but from that moment I recognized her as an ideal of so many young women who dream but do not dare to do the pioneering..."

On July 18, after two weeks, the Navy ordered the *Lexington* to return to the mainland, admitting "termination [of mission] without success." When the ship passed under the Golden Gate Bridge on its arrival in San Francisco, it lowered its colors to halfmast. The greatest air-sea search to that date, and perhaps since, was officially concluded. Unofficial searches have never ceased.

Only Amy Earhart knew the exact moment when she finally gave up hope of Amelia's survival and eventual return. As long as there was no funeral to attend, nor any grave to visit, she could believe that Amelia was just away on one of her trips, and when she returned the mystery of where she had been would be solved.

But her daughter was never seen again and no piece of the Electra was ever found. Only the legend remained alive.

TWENTY-THREE

The Living Legend of Amelia 1937-1982

For forty-five years the Earhart story came and went in print and on radio or television. Memorials in Amelia's honor were abundant, and included exhibits and scholarships; a mountain peak, a tidewater dam, a fountain, schools, streets, a hotel, an iris, a rose, a dahlia, and a tree, all named for her; plaques and markers at airports and on hangars; a commemorative airmail stamp issued by the United States Post Office; and on Howland Island the Earhart Memorial Light, a flashing beacon in mid-Pacific. Her idealized image became the subject of a cult for all people, male and female, young and old, in search of a heroic model, and her fame and fascination will continue, first because of her genuine achievements and second because her disappearance may never be conclusively explained.

"Whatever happened to Amelia Earhart?" was the logical continuation of the legend, generating its own power as a puzzle for casual fans and professional peers and as a pursuit for seekers of the truth. At the time there were those who "found" messages in bottles drifting at sea or washed up on beaches, and those who started rumors of her presence in various parts of the world. As late as 1970 a reticent New Jersey widow and former pilot was "unmasked" as Amelia Earhart living incognito as the result of an exchange between governments: her person for permission to keep Emperor Hirohito on the Japanese throne at the end of World War II. This theory was denied by the widow herself, who offered to present her fingerprints for comparison. Others to this day will look you in the eye and swear Amelia Earhart is living in Australia, Arizona, or New Mexico, or even as an amnesiac on a Pacific Island with her fisherman husband.

The rumors and speculations of capture and execution, of accident or suicide, the false hopes and false leads, the outright hoaxes, and even the mistakenly identified bones dug up on Saipan and later proved scientifically not to be Caucasian, only led to a prolongation of the fever to explain the disappearance.

The most persistent and consistent rumor held that Amelia Earhart and Fred Noonan either crashed or were shot down, and either died or were executed, while carrying out a secret spy mission on personal orders from President Roosevelt. If nothing tangible exists or has been revealed to prove he did, none exists to prove he didn't ask Amelia to overfly the area and garner what information about, and possible photographs of, airports and naval facilities she could. In spite of the great distances and the hazards, this would have been possible with additional equipment and adjustments to the Lockheed Electra, or with an exchange of planes accomplished secretly before she left New Guinea.

Whatever the truth, the search the Navy put on, and the recorded evidence of those aboard the Coast Guard cutter *Itasca* and other ships on station off Howland, and those people waiting on the island itself, who heard Amelia's voice and believed her to be approximately within one hundred miles of them at the last, still make it equally if not more reasonable to assume she ran out of fuel and crashed in their near vicinity. But capture and execution by the enemy is a more heroic and dramatic ending, and so the speculation persists.

Any number of serious attempts to discover what really happened took place before, during, and after World War II. American military forces were ordered to watch for information or relics of any kind as they fought their way up through the Pacific islands, and a good many GIs ran into natives who knew about or had heard about or had seen or thought they had seen a white lady flyer and a man with a bandage on his head. All this fitted in part with what Jacqueline Cochran believed she had "seen," the plane floating, Amelia alive and Fred unconscious from a head wound. Only she believed that after three days, the plane sank, carrying her friends with it. Nevertheless, as head of the Women's Air Force Service Pilots, the WASPs who ferried planes around the United States and to the European war zones, she made extensive inquiries and investigations when she entered Tokyo immediately after the Japanese surrender. She found nothing, however, to explain the disappearance of Amelia Earhart, and remained satisfied with her own extrasensory perceptions.

In 1960 Fred Goerner, a CBS newsman in San Francisco, with great encouragement from the late Admiral of the Fleet Chester W. Nimitz, began a prodigious and commendatory six-year search to substantiate the widely held belief that Amelia and Fred after capture had died on Saipan. Although he failed to do this conclusively, Goerner did discover the existence of classified United States Navy files that he believed proved the theory and possibly contained the location of her grave. These were not released to him, but in July 1967, they were opened to "discredit books and magazine articles which claimed Miss Earhart crashed on the island of Saipan and was executed by the Japanese as a spy." The official conclusion was that her plane "ran out of gas about 200 miles north of Howland Island and plunged into the sea." More specifically, the files contained no evidence that Miss Earhart "ever had any contact with the Japanese."

The extent of Roosevelt's involvement and interest in Amelia's round-the-world flight lies buried at Hyde Park and somewhere in the Pacific; and the final word to date belongs to the President's widow, who shortly before her death in 1962 told the pilot's sister that "Franklin and I loved Amelia too much to send her to her death..."

A rumor of suicide arises occasionally, and is only notable

because it so entirely misrepresents the character of Amelia Earhart. It claims that being fed up with her marriage and tired of empty fame, or having an unsatisfactory affair with some man, or not wanting to retire into the obscurity of a research program at Purdue University or to face the physical deterioration of age, or perhaps already suffering a terminal illness, Amelia chose to "pop off" voluntarily. No one with the remotest understanding of and appreciation for her integrity as a human being, a woman, and a pilot could believe such a false and especially malicious rumor. To be sure, she dreaded retirement and old age, and as she said often, "When I go, I'd like best to go in my plane. Quickly." Still, it is a canard to suggest she would kill herself and willy-nilly take along another person.

When Amelia disappeared, responsibility for Amy Earhart's welfare shifted to George Putnam. He professed to admire and respect his mother-in-law, but approval of "Dear Mother Earhart," as she suddenly became, did not prevent his administering AE's estate in ways different from what Amelia had intended. Her will was specific enough, leaving her personal effects to her husband, and the remainder to be held in trust, the net income to go to Amy in her lifetime, and after her death the principal to George outright. If he died first, then after Amy the income was to go to Muriel, and following her, to the Morrissey children. As executor and trustee with "absolute discretion," George persuaded the court that $125 a month was ample for an older lady living alone. At his death on January 4, 1950, in Trona, California, Amelia's estate was nearly exhausted, and Mrs. Earhart was living on approximately fifty to one hundred dollars a month. In time, the trust was dissolved, and friends and relatives took over her welfare.

For months and years, Amy Earhart kept her faith strong by denying all negative rumors and speculations. Amelia was simply unable to let anyone know where she was, and in time she would pop up and everything would revert to normal again. For two years she kept a suitcase packed with clothing, sunburn cream, and scissors to cut Amelia's hair whenever she was found. She was ready at any moment to go with any one of several pilots who offered to fly her anywhere to bring Amelia home.

On Amelia's fifty-sixth birthday, Amy declared positively in a Los Angeles *Times* interview that Amelia had been captured by the Japanese and taken to Tokyo, where she lost her life in an "arranged accident. I am sure there was a government mission involved in the flight," she added, "for Amelia explained there were some things she could not tell me." The source of this information was a mosaic of "reports, letters, conversations — bits of evidence and documentation" which she had been sent or had found, cut out of the newspapers, and saved over the years.

By then Amy was well into her eighties and inclined to lose her way if she took a notion to leave the house alone. Still sturdy though, a good walker, and one of the world's prolific correspondents, she lived with Muriel and her family in Medford. The two grandchildren were a joy, Muriel was a comfort, and Amy was gratified and stimulated to instant animation by the least sign of interest in the subject of Amelia. She retained an international celebrity status to her death in 1962, because she was "Mother Earhart" to innumerable young women whom she adopted and because her own devoted daughter had been the pioneer woman flyer Amelia Earhart.

Muriel, on the other hand, was able much sooner to accept the brutal reality that her sister was lost forever. Twenty-two days after the disappearance, she wrote Amy how wonderful it would be if AE brought "her own self home" for her birthday on July 24; but nine months later, she was of the opinion that everything considered, it seemed "better to face the situation and yield." She herself believed that "the plane must have crashed at once, and quickly and mercifully the water closed." It was perhaps the easiest way for her to cope with the overwhelming fact of Amelia's absence and the realization of how greatly she had depended on "our dear old grasser hop" for decisions, advice, and sisterly support whenever she wanted them, and sometimes when she didn't.

Having put off a career to raise her children, she wrote later of Amelia, "That she did not live to have a child of her own and to enjoy the honors she had earned is sad." Which missed the point entirely. Honors meant little to Amelia, her self-satisfaction was internal, the gratification of achievement at the moment of completion, not the external acclaim and award that came afterward. And only her own refusal to delay her career prevented her from having a child. Amelia's first priority *was* her career.

In time Muriel and Albert, whom she called "Chief," came to an accommodation; he was, after all, a good man with no vices. The children, David and Amy, continued to be her greatest joy as she completed her education and became an English teacher in Medford, where she still resides. For years, in addition to her own writing, she has furnished information, given speeches about, and attended various functions around the nation, in honored memory of her famous sister. More important to her, she has made her position as a notable and respected civic and social leader in her own community on her own account, not from behind the shadow of Amelia.

TWENTY · FOUR

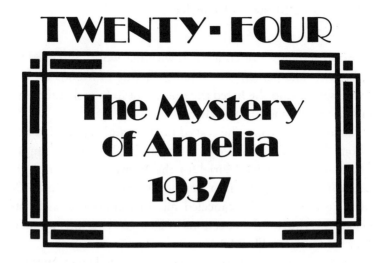

The Mystery of Amelia 1937

Because Amelia Earhart and other pilots dared to explore the skies, aviation developed as a vital commercial venture which led to technological, medical, and biological advances of benefit to everyone. Because of her and the Ninety-Nines, women went into a field earlier thought to be reserved for men, and equal rights for women gained further status as a social necessity. And because of her husband, a legend flourished and many people worshiped an image of cool perfection.

But Amelia Earhart was not always cool and she was not always perfect. She was real, and a part of her was as down-to-earth as anyone. At times she was subject to contradictory impulses which moved her to apparently inconsistent attitudes and actions, and almost without fail she was ill after periods of great emotional and physical stress. Ferociously protective of her independence, she still needed to be an influential participant in a close family situation, as well as member of a professional group such as the Ninety-Nines, the women's flying association of which she was the first president. Zonta International, the association for business and professional women, was the only nonflying organization she joined voluntarily, although she was an honorary member of many other groups and associations. She was so profoundly private and solitary, however, that only occasionally did she make the effort to be physically present at meetings, or to take part in group activities not concerned with her work. She liked best to be with one person or a small gathering of friends for good conversation, and she hated the time spent in formal entertaining in her own home, or anywhere.

As much as anyone, she craved the love and approval of those whom she loved or wanted to please and only rarely to impress. The competition with Muriel for the attention of their mother was unmistakable, and in a stepmotherly contest with the first Mrs. Putnam, Amelia canceled all engagements and devoted herself to vying for the affections of George's two sons whenever they visited from Florida.

It is fair to say these two examples represented an ego necessity for Amelia: she unfailingly wanted to be what others wanted or expected her to be. At the same time they were only other instances of the compulsion to be responsible and "do the right thing" for those in her care or for those whom she cared about. When she gave her love it was never out of conscious self-interest, but never given wholly either. Always she kept a distance, sometimes warm and sometimes chilly, between herself and other people. When she admired and respected someone it was natural to be pleasing or even ingratiating, particularly if she could win a favor for her consuming passion, aviation, and the stubborn ambition it bred in her. Or even when no favor was involved, a desire not to be remiss or negligent in any respect, even a slight social convention, could make her write long apologies for embarrassments she could not have prevented. One went to Anne Lindbergh for the "Lady Lindy" nickname, and another to Eleanor Roosevelt for what Amelia called the "starvation interview."

As a feminist, Amelia could still understand how some women out of fear or financial dependency accepted housewifery as the only career they could or would aspire to. She could not or would not believe that other women preferred the role of wife and mother, not because they were unendowed with either career talent or ambition but because they genuinely enjoyed baby-tending and housework, and that still other women happily combined the two. With Amelia it was all or nothing.

Although her most passionate anger was against war, her honesty also recalled how in Toronto she was "excited and joyfully aware of [war's] romance." As she wrote in *The Home Magazine* of August 1935, "If women go to war, along with their men, the men are just going to hate it! If they hate it enough, perhaps they will give up wars altogether."

Drafting women was not even a possibility then; furthermore, she was not so naïve as to believe her own theory. She had a strong feeling that men would "rather vacate the arena of war altogether than share it with women..." She agreed that war had a meaning and object when it was a "national emergency in which no one is exempt," adding that if asked to serve, she would "force [herself] to languish in jail..."

Amelia had no patience for human inefficiency, indecision, incompetence, or indifference, and she was equally intolerant of professional exaggeration or glorification of her own abilities and achievements. She had been an all but untrained aide at a military hospital in World War I, not a "war nurse," and she was not a genuine poet, only a scribbler of verse. She was not the only contemporary female to advocate feminine rights or to be a pioneer in the history of aviation. Better than anyone, she knew the reality behind the myth which was so luminous and so capable of bringing in funds to pay for more flights. As long as the puffery functioned financially without hurting anyone, she permitted it to continue without realizing that occasionally even she forgot which was the blind side of the image.

In an age when most girls and young women customarily dreamed of men as marriage prospects, Amelia was off competing with her sister pilots in the "Powder Puff Derby" or selling aviation safety to housewives so they would let their husbands make business trips by air. After the *Friendship* flight in 1928 as a passenger, Amelia dreamed of equaling or surpassing the professional achievements of Colonel Charles A. Lindbergh, the world's greatest male flyer. Her instinct was sounder than she realized; they could have been twins. The physical resemblance was obvious from the beginning, and their daring and courage, and the vision to seek and reach objectives beyond the aspirations and capabilities of ordinary people set Amelia Earhart and Charles A. Lindbergh apart.

Significantly, Amelia had hoped for May 20–21, 1932, for the first solo transatlantic crossing by a woman, and if the weather had failed her, the shine might have been off her personal triumph. Five years before, on May 20–21, 1927, Lindbergh had made his solo flight across the North Atlantic.

The two crossed paths at public functions, and on occasion in private, as when the balloonist Auguste Piccard visited the Putnams from Belgium and the Lindberghs were invited to Rye to meet him. Each worked hard to make a success of TAT, which later became TWA, and the two couples were guests together once or twice at the Los Angeles residence of Jack Maddux, head of TAT's western division.

For the most part, however, while Charles was away exploring and surveying commercial air routes in exotic and isolated places, Amelia was breaking flight records, appearing on lecture platforms, and setting feminine precedents. Although he carefully considered whether going somewhere would draw the press, she went everywhere regardless. From observing how his eyes turned icy and his lips tightened in angry disdain when he was confronted by newsmen who couldn't ignore his fame but had no desire to soothe his outrage, Amelia made herself endure without so much as a grimace the persistent pressure, impertinences, and misstatements of the journalists. With crowds she was almost as amenable, only infrequently shrinking away physically when someone pressed too close.

After the Honolulu to Oakland triumph, she decided to match another Lindbergh record. In December of 1927, the Colonel had flown from Washington, D.C., down the eastern coast of Mexico as far as Tampico, where he became lost. In due time the first person to solo from the United States to Mexico City arrived. Very late.

Amelia left Burbank on a midnight in April 1935, and traced her course over the Gulf of California, turning east at Mazatlán. She expected to arrive in the Mexican capital at one o'clock in the afternoon. At that hour, with no sign of a city ahead, she landed near a village and conferred in sign language with the natives. Then she took off to fly the last fifty miles to Mexico City, where she arrived very late indeed, but still the first person to solo from Los Angeles to Mexico City. If she had known of it, Amelia might have been mildly amused at the thought of these two flyers losing their way to the same destination. More likely she would have started at once to determine how and why such a thing could happen and to make recommendations for its never happening again. Had Charles Lindbergh known of it, he would have reacted the same way.

Whether Amelia realized it or not, competition with Lindbergh was like competing with herself because of the manner in which they thought and planned and sought out the unknown and hurried toward danger instead of away from it. In *Hour of Gold, Hour of Lead*, Anne Morrow Lindbergh wrote, "The biggest surprise, though, was Amelia Earhart...She is the most amazing person — just as tremendous as C., I think. It startles me how much alike they are in breadth...She has the clarity of mind, impersonal eye, coolness of temperament, balance of a scientist..."

Amelia had all these, and she as well as Charles had also that special quality of leadership which captures the popular imagination and inspires unswerving allegiance and devotion. Because of events and the nature of his work, Lindbergh's appeal to the public was finally turned against him, many people thought unfairly. But Amelia's public never failed her. To see her run a comb through her short tousled hair as she popped out of her plane upon landing, to catch a glimpse of her, coltish and youthful but completely composed in a long evening gown, to see her grin cheerfully or hear her infectious laughter was never to forget her. Those too young at the time heard and read and dreamed about her and never forgot her either. Nor is it difficult to understand why she is as greatly loved and as famous today as in her own time and down the years since she vanished.

Amelia Earhart was clear as glass and cloudy as milk at the same time, and she was marked for greatness. She rarely failed either in public or in private to live up to what she demanded of herself. She would not compromise with integrity, she did not quail before danger, and she brought honor by word and deed to her sex, her country, her kin, and herself.

RECORDS SET BY AMELIA EARHART

1922	October	Long Beach, California, Airshow	Altitude, 14,000 ft
1928	June 17–18	North Atlantic	First woman to cross the Atlantic Ocean by air
	September	Transcontinental	First woman's solo round trip
1929	November 22	Los Angeles	Speed record for women
1930	June 28	Detroit, Michigan	Speed records for 100 km; and for 100 km with payload of 500 km
1931	April 8	Pitcairn Field, Willow Grove, Pennsylvania	Broke altitude record for autogiros at 15,000 ft, and then broke this new record by going to 18,415 ft on the same day
1932	May 20–21	North Atlantic	First woman to cross the Atlantic Ocean solo. First person to cross the Atlantic Ocean twice
	August 24–25	Transcontinental	Women's nonstop transcontinental speed record, Los Angeles to Newark, 19 hr, 5 min
1933	July 7–8	Transcontinental	Broke own record made the previous year, 17 hr, 7½ min
1935	January 11–12	Honolulu–Oakland	First person to fly Hawaii to California. First person to solo anywhere in the Pacific. First person to solo over both Atlantic and Pacific Oceans
	April 19–20	Mexico	First person to solo from Los Angeles to Mexico City
	May 8	Newark	First person to solo from Mexico to Newark
1937	March 17	Oakland–Honolulu	Record for east to west crossing, 15 hr, 52 min
	June 1–July 2	Around the world at the Equator	Not completed

SOURCES

Unpublished

The letters of Amelia Earhart Putnam

Correspondence preserved by Amy Otis Earhart, including letters from Muriel Earhart Morrissey and from George Palmer Putnam

Three reminiscences by Muriel Earhart Morrissey

"Notes Prepared by A.O.E."

Answers to nearly 150 questions put to Mrs. Earhart by persons unknown

Published

News clippings not identified, preserved by Mrs. Earhart

News articles:

Allen, C. B., "Miss Earhart Not Above Greasy Clothes and Airport Diner," New York *Herald Tribune*, June 6, 1937.

Briand, Paul L., Jr., "Was She on a Secret Mission?" *Ms.*, September 1976.

Hamill, Pete, "The Cult of Amelia Earhart," *Ms.*, September 1976.

Mabie, Janet, "At Home with Amelia Earhart," *Christian Science Monitor*, January 9, 1935.

————"A Bird's-Eye View of Fashions," *ibid.*, February 7, 1934.

————"Girl Who Flew the Atlantic Discovers Fun in Little Ways," *ibid.*, July 27, 1932.

————"Now She Has a Treasure Chest," *ibid.*, January 25, 1936.

National Geographic Society, "The Society's Special Medal Awarded to Amelia Earhart," *The National Geographic Magazine*, September 1932.

Putnam, Amelia Earhart, "Are American Women Holding Aviation Back?" *Liberty*, February 13, 1937.

————"Draft Women for War," *The Home Magazine*, August 1935.

Railey, Hilton H., "Chance Sent Amelia Earhart on First Ocean Voyage," Philadelphia *Evening Bulletin*, September 10, 1936.

Newspapers identified

Atchison, Kansas, *Daily Globe*

Berkeley, California, *Daily Gazette*

SOURCES

Newspapers identified (continued)

Boston *Globe, Herald Traveler,* and *Evening American; Christian Science Monitor*

Kansas City *Star*

Los Angeles *Times; Evening Herald and Express;* and *Examiner*

Miami *Herald*

New York *Herald Tribune; Times* and *Times Book Review*

Oakland, California, *Tribune*

Sacramento *Bee*

San Francisco *Chronicle*

Books

Burke, John, *Winged Legend.* New York: G. P. Putnam's Sons, 1970; Berkeley Medallion Edition, October 1976.

Gill, Brendan, *Lindbergh Alone.* New York: Harcourt Brace Jovanovich, 1977.

Goerner, Fred G., *The Search for Amelia Earhart.* Garden City, N.Y.: Doubleday & Company, Inc., 1966.

Lindbergh, Anne Morrow, *Hour of Gold, Hour of Lead.* New York: Harcourt Brace Jovanovich, 1973.

Lindbergh, Charles A., *The Spirit of St. Louis.* New York: Charles Scribner's Sons, 1953.

————*We.* New York: G. P. Putnam's Sons, 1927.

Morrissey, Muriel Earhart, *Courage Is the Price.* Wichita, Kans.: McCormick-Armstrong Publishing Division, 1963.

Putnam, Amelia Earhart, *Last Flight* (arranged by George Palmer Putnam). New York: Harcourt, Brace & Company, 1937.

————*The Fun of It.* New York: Harcourt, Brace and Company, 1932; reprint edition, Academy Press, Ltd., Chicago, 1977.

————*20 Hrs. 40 Min.* New York: G. P. Putnam's Sons, 1928.

Putnam, George Palmer, *Soaring Wings.* New York: Harcourt, Brace & Company, 1939.

ACKNOWLEDGMENT

I wish to express my most sincere gratitude to Mrs. Muriel Earhart Morrissey. Immediately upon learning that the letters from Amelia to their mother had been found, she gave her permission freely to write the book, offered her full assistance, and sent me a copy of her own *Courage Is the Price*. On the flyleaf she wrote her best wishes "as you seek to make Amelia fly again."

JEAN L. BACKUS
Kensington, California
January 1982

629.13092   Backus, Jean L.
Bac   Letters from Amelia,
             1901-1937

9,18

DATE DUE		
DEC 02 '86		
JAN 3 '87		
NOV 24 '87		
DEC 16 '87		
JAN 04 '88		